THE LEADEN-SKY YEARS OF WORLD WAR II

ISBN: 960-226-609-0

EFSTATHIADIS GROUP S.A.
88 Drakontos Str.,
104 42 Athens
tel.: ++3210 5154 650,
fax: ++3210 5154 657
e-mail: efgroup@otenet.gr
GREECE

Printed and bound in Greece

Cover design: *Elina Logotheti*
Photo: *PANAYOTIS FARANTAKIS*

KIMON FARANTAKIS

THE LEADEN-SKY YEARS OF WORLD WAR II

Diary Notes of a Schoolboy in Occupied Crete

translated from Greek
by
P. David Seaman, Ph.D.
Northern Arizona University

Athens, Greece

To the memory of those who took a stand
with Greek and humanitarian soul
in the midst of atrocities of war

CONTENTS

INTRODUCTORY NOTE

The events described in this book actually happened. They are based on diary notes made by the author when he was 12 and 13 years old, giving vent to his everyday thoughts and feelings during the German occupation of Crete. Fortunately he preserved the notes, and fifty years later edited and rewrote some of them for publication in Greece.

These published accounts are therefore the writing of a well-educated adult, finally sharing his boyhood reactions to stressful wartime experiences. The incredible hardships are often described in almost poetic language, but language which will communicate to readers on several different levels. Those who have suffered through wars will relate with empathy; those who have not will have a deeper understanding and be better able to count their blessings after reading this book.

The original version was published in Modern Greek as Ta Xronia Tou Xalkinou Ouranou (The Years of the Copper Sky), *Zaxaropoulos Company, Athens, 1993. It was read in Greek by the undersigned, who urged that it be translated for a wider English-language audience. This translation was done with the active cooperation of the author.*

As in the original, some changes have been made in chronology, and in certain names of places and persons. This is done to avoid embarrassing those who survived, or the memory of those who did not.

The accounts given here concentrate on the setting of one village in Crete and in part of the time period involving the tragedy of war. They are intended to help show how these terrible years were reflected in the eyes of a child, and how they made a lasting imprint on that person's life.

For the convenience of those not familiar with the long history of Greece, or of World War II, this edition provides a relevant brief historic summary. In addition, an Epilogue newly prepared by the author gives interesting glimpses into the later lives of a few of the survivors.

Any discrepancies between the original Greek version and this English translation are the translator's fault, not the author's.

P. David Seaman, Ph.D.
Northern Arizona University

PROLOGUE

Greek Historical Background. Greece has long been a crossroads for trade and for the development and exchange of new ideas – such as democracy.

Through great strides in philosophy, this small country brought the light of reason to the world, and through the development of many arts and sciences laid the foundations of the western civilization.

Down through the ages, Greece has also been the scene of countless military conflicts. These were described in ancient times by the legendary Greek poet Homer in his Iliad, by Herodotus, Thucydides, and Xenephon in their Histories, and in more recent times by numerous other historians.

For the past two thousand years, the inhabitants of Greece have been subjected to almost continuous attack, occupation or enslavement by outside forces, including the Romans, Goths, Huns, Arabs, Slavs, Bulgars, Venetians, Franks, Genoese, Ottoman Turks, and most recently the Germans in World War II.

The Turks controlled much of Greece for 500 years, and even today many Greek villages are often referred to by two different names, one Greek and one a familiar Turkish designation.

Through all these hardships the Greeks did not lose their vitality nor their identity as Greeks. They did not succumb to despair nor adopt their oppressors' language and culture, which often happens in similar circumstances. Close-knit ties to family and village, and to the Greek Orthodox Church, reinforced the sense of Greekness and strengthened the individualism which is still today a marked characteristic of Greek personality. This is frequently reflected in everyday Greek life and in the turbulent individualistic politics of the country.

Thanks to some seventeenth-century setbacks to Ottoman aggression, and to the French Revolution in the late eighteenth century, the Greeks were inspired to revolt against their Turkish overlords. After a few preliminary uprisings, the successful Greek rebellion against the Turks began in earnest in 1821. With some outside help from England, France, and Russia, hostilities concluded in 1827, with establishment of a free Greek state under the tutelage of these three larger powers. At that time the nation was considerably smaller than present-day Greece.

Additional lands and populations were gradually added over the next century or so, usually with multi-nation agreements after various wars, and frequently involving exchanges of populations. For example, after the Turkish destruction of the Greek-populated Smyrna in Asia Minor, one-and-one-half-million Greeks left Turkey for Greece and a half-million Turks left Greece for Turkey.

Crete, where the events recorded in this book occurred, officially became a part of modern Greece in 1913. But the Greek language and culture had already been predominant there for over five thousand years!

Because of effective Turkish and British opposition, Cyprus has never been allowed to join Greece, even though 80% of its population is Greek. The latest addition to Greece was when Italy ceded the Dodecanese Islands – including Rhodes – to Greece after World War II.

World War II. In terms of destruction of lives and property the Second World War was the costliest in history.

After the end of World War I in 1918, several nations – notably Germany, Italy, and Japan – were disgruntled with the terms of the treaty settlements. Less than twenty years later, the League of Nations had failed to become an influence for world peace, and the United States was taking a position isolating it from European concerns. At the same time that many of the European nations were squabbling among themselves, Germany had regained strength and was busily rearming.

Under the leadership of Adolf Hitler, in the

late 1930s a flurry of cooperative and non-aggression agreements were signed. These pacts were later changed or ignored at Hitler's convenience. The result was a group of Axis Powers consisting of Germany, Japan, Italy, and several smaller countries who were persuaded or coerced into joining.

Hitler moved first against Austria, in 1938, then Czechoslovakia, Poland, and several other countries. Holland and Belgium fell in May 1940 and France in June 1940. Hitler hoped to conquer Britain by cutting off their supplies of food, oil, and other materials. He initiated submarine warfare in the Atlantic and began plans to gain control of the Mediterranean, North Africa and the Middle East.

At first Hitler persuaded the USSR to be on the side of the Axis, with promises of non-aggression and territorial benefits. But in June 1941 he attacked Russia in what turned out to be a very costly campaign.

Japan signed a non-aggression pact with the USSR, and concentrated on attacking islands in the

Pacific. The Japanese sneak attack on Pearl Harbor in Hawaii, on December 7, 1941, was a strategic mistake. The United States, which had been following an isolationist policy while quietly helping its friends in the Atlantic, now became much more active in the war and in rearmament efforts.

The United States, as part of the Allied Powers, made a strategic decision to at first make mainly defensive stands in the Pacific while concentrating most of its war effort on defeating Hitler in Europe. (The heroic efforts of the Allied Powers in the Pacific, culminating in the surrender of Japan in August 1945, are not treated here.)

The Mediterranean Theater of War. In 1940, with most of central and northern Europe under his control, Hitler turned some of his attention to the Balkans as a means of clearing a supply route to the Axis efforts in the Mediterranean.

Allied defense of Africa, including Egypt and the Suez Canal, was dependent upon British control of the Mediterranean Sea. This was crucial for pro-Western Greece, too, which clearly could not long withstand simultaneous attacks by land, sea, and air. However, except for Gibraltar, the British did not have any land bases in the western Mediterranean. Italy controlled most of that area, as well as the Dodecanese Islands in the eastern Mediterranean. British offers of defensive cooperation fell on deaf ears in most of the eastern Mediterranean countries, except for Greece.

Hitler, while he continued to make overtures of peace and friendship to Greece, had assigned control of the Mediterranean to the Italians under Mussolini. However, in September 1940 Mussolini was unsuccessful in an attack on British-occupied Egypt.

On October 28, 1940, Mussolini attacked Greece across the Albanian border. At the time, Greece had 8 million inhabitants, compared to Italy's 45 million. Nevertheless, the Italian troops were routed and severely defeated as winter set in.

In April 1941, Germany simultaneously attacked Yugoslavia and Greece. The foot soldiers and older equipment were no match for the modern German panzer divisions, and the Greek mainland fell by the end of April. (The king escaped to Crete, then to Cairo, and later to London where he set up a Greek government in exile.)

After the fall of the Greek mainland, the Germans repeatedly bombed the British and Greek installations in Crete. Early on the morning of May 20, 1941, the Germans launched a paratroop-led invasion of Crete. Pitched battles raged for one week, until British troops were evacuated from the southern coast, with great loss of life on both sides.

The freedom-loving inhabitants of Crete did not take easily to the yoke of occupation, and many set up underground resistance groups in the mountains. However, the German treatment was harsh in this important island, with severe retribution for the slightest infractions.

The events described in this book stretch from May 20, 1943, exactly two years after the German invasion of Crete, through late August 1944, four months after the Allied invasion of Europe which culminated in the unconditional German surrender in May 1945.

Diary Notes:
1943

DIARY NOTES: 1943

20 May

AVLOCHI is a small, artificial-looking vale outside our village.

Down from the large stone fence to the east, when it rains a large dome-like cataract forms. It deposits in its flat cavity a pliable layer of pure white clay. When I am here alone I like to use the clay to make human shapes – an antidote to the never-ending loneliness.

Today I was sitting on the rock where I have sat countless times, molding the clay and thinking to myself . . .

It was at this very spot that Vasilis and I were

playing two years ago, the morning the German invasion began.

At first one could hear a deep roar, like the roaring of the distant sea. This quickly changed into an explosive drone of machines far more intense than what I had just gotten accustomed to.

A fearsome sound-arc covered half the dome of the sky northwards and hurried along towards the other signs on the horizon. The sound intensified incessantly and converged from all directions, overwhelming every retreat in the natural universe.

For the first time I understood that this noise alone could be a threat to life and even to the earth itself.

That gave me an eerie feeling which caused me to cringe and shake uncontrollably, so much that I ran the risk of dying on the spot.

In that deplorable new state I lifted my eyes. The airplanes cast a shadow above me over a large part of the sky. I saw that they had begun to drop parachutes like snowflakes, and were turning back to strafe and to drop bombs, a pandemonium – the end of the world.

The memory of that morning – two years have passed now – jarred my nerves. I noticed that I had crushed between my palms the small clay bust which I had carefully made just a little earlier today.

But I collected myself quickly. I looked sadly at the broken shape and shuddered. It is obvious that I still haven't recovered from the experience of that terrible day two years ago.

28 May

MY MOTHER'S village lies deep in the mountains. The day before yesterday they held a memorial service there for those who had been killed. My mother got me up while it was still night and we walked three hours to get to the service.

We arrived a little before it was ending. At that time the church was filled with people, disorderly, and everyone crying out.

A grandfather was scolding his grandchild who was sluggishly eating a piece of the communion bread: «Eat it quickly, so the priest may give you another piece, you blockhead».

In the back could be heard a groaning, all with one voice: «The bastard Death gathers the best of the flowers».

At that moment the priest genuflected before the holy altar. He did it in a disorderly way, clumsily, and bending so much that he seemed to be leaning heavily over plowed ground in his effort to plant a tree.

While he was hunched over there and stammering a prayer, a long-bearded man shouted at him, all crazy and wild-eyed: «Father, why don't you call a curse down upon those German dogs».

The priest glared at him, and then responded, still kneeling there: «Cursed be the evil which lurks in a person and makes him behave like a scorpion and a wolf».

29 May

EVER SINCE they laid the minefields in the plain, two years ago, the village's land has been limited. In the area that we are allowed to use, the soil is becoming poorer, because there isn't any more fertilizer. Less dung is available since they requisitioned half of the village's animals to feed the occupation troops.

Some of the farmers, quite concerned, turned to the neighboring hills. With hoes, pickaxes, and plows they ripped up stones and densely-growing bushes in order to increase the cultivatable land. The landscape changed in appearance.

For two years the land yielded crops. But slowly the rains eroded the soft soil and opened up little rivulets. On the steeper slopes the roots of the trees were exposed so that they dried out and waved – tatters blowing in the wind.

This year, from very early on, the leaves on the olive trees were curled up in little grooves, and being few and far between, left the tree branches almost bare. Trees and bushes showed their struggle to cling to life in the depleted soil.

Very early this morning we went to check the condition of the new plantings in our own field at Arkaloplagia.

The crops are depressingly poor. The wheat is stubby, yellow, and looks like it will produce a miserable crop. Some wheat is not ripening at all, and is drying on the stalk.

Where heads of wheat are appearing, they're only growing from one side – two or three scraggly seeds and two or three bugs – stalks of hunger.

30 May

IT WAS our teacher's idea for us kids to go to Melissourio, to the annual memorial service for Photis. He was the twelve-year-old boy who lost his life at Maleme during the German invasion.

«The soul of a child wants to sense children around it. It wants those who can laugh and still hope, even though the world is mired down in blood like we are...», said the teacher sadly, and no one could find any reason to argue.

On the day of the German invasion, Photis was traveling to Hania in a buggy, with sixteen-year-old Paul as driver.

The swarm of German airplanes caught them at Kondomari, just outside of Maleme.

The pandemonium erupting from the engines, the machine guns and the bombs from the airplanes, frightened their young jet-black horse. The animal bolted and began to gallop crazily on the rough gravel road, with the buggy bouncing in the air like a small boat on a stormy sea.

The young people jumped from the buggy and sought refuge in a nearby orchard. It was their bad luck, however, that the field was muddy, really deep, and with their first step they sank in up to their knees.

With a desperate lunge, Paul – who in addition had taken a bullet in his leg – managed to grab a low-hanging branch near him and to pull himself out of the mire. Photis was still stuck, even deeper in the mud.

A prisoner there of his fate, he saw his companion about to flee like a frightened rabbit, and began to call to him desperately:

«Help, Paul! Don't leave me alone. I can't move. Don't...»

But the only thing Paul found the courage to do was to turn his head and say to him:

«Be quiet, or the airplanes will hear us and kill us on the spot».

Then he disappeared – a whirlwind behind the reeds.

With a face flushed red as fire and with the terror of death in his eyes, Photis continued to call and to search around him for some evidence of life. But this newly experienced destruction had driven away men, birds, and animals from the universe, and had suddenly changed it into a desert of death.

Eight days later, the dust of battle had settled a little and people came back to the village. They found the boy curled up in the muddy field, dead. Anyway, there was not a single wound on his whole body.

31 May

TODAY two British prisoners, exhausted from hunger, passed along our road. They had them on an open army vehicle, with chains on their legs.

As soon as the vehicle stopped they greeted us with upraised thumbs – the sign of courage. They asked if they could perhaps have an onion to eat along with the fat from a sardine tin which they – pale and disgusted – passed back and forth to each other, dipping their fingers and licking them.

George Digalis gave them a handful of onions and a large dark rusk, dry as charcoal.

One of them tried to break the rusk into two pieces, but couldn't do it.

«If you can't chew it you'll have to eat plain chocolate», old George Digalis teased them, and laughed cheerfully.

And they laughed shyly, like helpless children laugh when they know they are being teased and that they are loved.

The German soldier who was guarding them–

very young, almost a child – showed his gun and made a sour-looking face which displayed no usual human emotion, neither love nor hate. It was more like a strange fear. I think I have seen that sort of fear in animals who have gotten sick from rabies and have an overwhelming premonition of death. They try to bite whatever they find in front of them, simply because they want to escape the feeling of death which has taken hold of them. But their disease isn't going away until they themselves die.

On the way home I kept thinking about the scene with the military vehicle. It seems to me that the most pitiful of all was the German fellow. I had a picture in my mind's eye of his expression, childlike and disheartened. So much so that if I met him again I would dare to invite him to play cops-and-robbers and quoits in the neighborhood play areas. I had the strange feeling that only something very simple, very human, like the outstretched hand of a child, could heal his inner wounds.

2 June

AT ANGALI, the Germans together with a local fisherman used dynamite on a large school of *mourmouria* fish. The shallow area near shore was silver-colored from the killed fish.

When their boat left it was loaded to the gunwales. But here and there were still some fish – silvery lightning – at the bottom of the ledge near the drop-off into deeper water.

We kids, four of us, took a boat and tried to gather some of the fish. But our arms were thin and weak from hunger, and the water was deep. So we couldn't control the harpoon, not even two of us together.

Suddenly a husky young German who was swimming near us grabbed hold of our boat and jumped in. He took the harpoon and began to spear the fish. He did it so easily that you might say he was writing letters on the rippled lines of the sandy bottom.

While he was harpooning, we boys were hiding half the fish here and there in the corners of the boat, because we believed he would take all the fish when he left.

Ashore, he bent over and removed the fish we had hidden, and spread them out with the other fish, on the deck of the boat. More than thirty splendid *mourmouria* fish! Then he made signs that he was giving all the fish to us as a present, saluted us and left.

On the rocks of the seashore we danced and laughed like monkeys.

5 June

YESTERDAY a man was killed while secretly releasing «Teller» land-mines. Russos was a good young fellow with strong hands, with which he descended into the deepest wells and climbed the tallest trees.

The explosion blew him to bits. What was left of his body they brought back in a small basket, wrapped with a white cloth filled with stains from the fluids of what remained of the youthful burned body.

I have seen many who died or were killed, but that was terrible.

Also terrible was the dirge of his mother, who is a fervent lamenter. I was able to write down some of her words, coming from the wild torrent of pain which welled up from within her and wouldn't stop.

Russos, don't make jokes and break my heart.

These drops of blood and pieces of flesh are not you.

You fill up the seas when you go fishing.

You change mountains into horses to ride them to festivals.

In July you are coolness and in the winter you are sunshine.

No, the cliffs are not crumbling, the sea is not emptying out.

The stars don't lose their light in a windstorm.

Come, our friends are standing, our own people are waiting.

They expect you to speak a word, my sorrow, my joy, my eagle.

8 June

FOR TWO OR THREE days now I have been trying to improve the light from my oil lamp, using various techniques. The light is so weak that it tires my eyes and makes me dizzy when I study in the evening for my tests.

I made a lampshade from white paper and with a wire tripod propped it up above the lamp to reflect the light downward. At first it worked fine. However, it wasn't long before the smoke from the lamp blackened the paper. And besides that, the paper gradually began to wrinkle up, showing that it was about to catch on fire. So I threw it away.

I lit some leftover beeswax candles given to me by Manolis, the church warden, but I threw them away quickly because they stank and made me nauseous.

I tried other things, too. I changed the height of the box which I was using for a lampstand. I changed wicks and lamps. Finally, I settled on a piece of cardboard, which I bent into a curve, and then whitened it with lime. I stood it upright behind the lamp, and thus I have a little better light.

Weakened by the long-term weariness of these days, and from hunger, I don't have much energy for studying in the evening. As soon as the dim flame of the lamp flickers, I feel sleepy and there spreads through my body a sweet drug, almost sensuous. But I really want to study. If only I had a good light!

This evening I am looking at the stars, and grumbling. Why don't they give off more light! I would like to have somewhere to complain, someone to scold for that inadequate situation.

Within me is a growing awareness that nothing is valid now. Neither logic nor a moral system. Let the theologians talk. The world seems to be torn down, and life is crawling under the ruins.

11 June

THREE OR FOUR craftsmen, skilled woodworkers and stone masons, escaped yesterday from Menies, on Cape Spathas, and returned to the village by night.

We heard how the Germans kept them there two whole years to keep them from giving pertinent information about the fortification efforts in that area. They even forced them to work alone and not talk with each other. They had warned them that if anyone was caught talking, they would cut out his tongue.

All those who were gathered around to greet them were horrified. Their eyes were strange, detached from their souls, like beads bouncing around in muddy water.

Dimitris, our neighbor, is the most shattered of all. His whole body shudders when he talks and tells us how his heart was pounding continually, ready to collapse. It was said that he was not able to speak endearingly to his children, nor to touch his wife. He kept begging them to close the windows, and strained his ears at every little sound like a hunted animal.

Today they asked Father Michael from Potamida to come give a blessing. The large-bodied white-haired priest swept into the house with a Bible under his arm and pulled up his sleeves with such energy that you would think he was coming in to start a fight. He told Dimitris to bow his head, and immediately began to read an exorcism with frightful words. His expression was threatening, wild.

After a moment Dimitris broke into a wailing cry with words filled with complaint: «Father Michael, I am not crazy, I am not crazy I tell you. I am not demon-possessed. I am dead. They took away my voice and I died. Stop these exorcisms and read me something about resurrection if you want to bring me back to life».

The priest trembled. For a moment there was a deathlike silence. Then he regained his composure and began in soothing tones to chant the «Resurrection Day».

12 June

JUST RECENTLY a pair of hooter birds built a nest in the top of the almond tree in our garden. With quick turning of their necks and their eyes, they seem to be surveying the whole world.

The differences every minute in their flitting around and their great variety of chirping day by day begin to make more sense. It seems to me that I am beginning to understand something of their fascinating language, the first and most valuable language in life.

With their constant moving and incessant noise, in just a few days the little birds gave the impression that this little corner of the world belongs completely to them.

Today there appeared in the vicinity a huge raven, with lustrous feathers like polished ebony, with all the majesty of Death in his self-assured presence.

With perfect form he glided through the trees, and let out a raucous call, an ugly frightening croak. This considerably quieted the torrent of chirping which filled the olive groves all around us.

The hooter birds stretched their necks in alarm, instantly flew into the air with harsh dragged-out clacking chirps - something like the sound of grinding steel plates in a gear box - and rushed at the intruding bird of prey.

Taken by surprise, the raven turned somersaults in the air to escape the pecking of the hooter birds.

The metallic trilling of the smaller birds, which became more piercing with each new assault, filled the startled raven with panic.

The commotion only stopped when the raven disappeared deep into the canyon to the south.

I was waiting to see the hooter birds who returned flying low over the fields with light melodious chirping.

That battle appeared important to me. It was a victory over death, and it steadied somewhat my faltering belief in the power of life.

17 June

ON SATURDAY Theoharis, my best friend, was badly burned with gunpowder, and now I learn that he may die.

He had filled his pockets with gunpowder bars, used for artillery primers, which sizzle and pop – like an enraged viper – when they catch fire.

He was lighting them to entertain and to scare the other, smaller kids. But somehow, no one understands exactly how, the ones he was carrying in his pockets caught fire and ruined his body.

The women of the neighborhood rushed horrified to the scene, calling out sharply to bring butter to daub on the wounds and clean sheets to wrap the burned body, and shouting for the men to send for the doctor, or a midwife if necessary.

And the kids broke down and were babbling incoherently.

The neighborhood took on the look of a flock of goats which had had a starving vulture dart right into the middle of the flock.

It seems unbelievable to me that such a small episode, a game, would snuff out an existence. Is it really possible that Time would consider as insignificant and incidental the large factor which is called Man?

19 June

ANOTHER strangely bitter thing happened this evening. My aunt, who has a flock, gave me a small piece of cheese. I clasped it in my hand and ran to eat it in the house.

My father was standing at the door of our house. He saw me come up and asked what I was holding. I quickly stuck the cheese in my pocket and said, «Nothing», shifty-eyed and frightened.

My father's face reddened. He smiled with a sorrowful expression on his face and said to me, «Are you afraid I'll take it from you? Don't be afraid». And he is such a proud person!

But he didn't understand. Even he made a mistake for once. The cheese was moldy, miserable in appearance, and hard as a rock. My only concern was that he would make me throw it away. But how could I explain all that to him?

Anyway, his voice had an unfathomably deep grieving in it, which for hours now has left me no peace. I can't sleep, either. That's why I got up and am writing these lines.

Never before had I imagined that this strong man could feel grief.

I went outside and looked at the sky with anxiety. There are some times that, without a specific reason, my soul leaves me. And I – an empty vessel – want to run behind her to bring her back. But I haven't the slightest idea where she went.

22 June

FOR MANY DAYS now I've been trying and finally I hit upon a way to make a rifle, a real rifle.

I carved a small rifle butt from a fig-tree branch. On top I stuck a firing pin, and a straight tube for a gun barrel. The firing pin is armed with a small wooden bar, which sticks out towards the bottom and also serves as the trigger.

I feel such great excitement that I have run through most of the village, showing it to the kids and shooting it to show its effectiveness.

The kids try not to look excited. They try to examine the gun calmly. But they don't fool me. I see clearly their red cheeks and their eyes moist from surprise. They didn't expect this accomplishment from such a quiet boy as I am.

This insignificant invention greatly boosts my self-confidence. Now I look at my hands with some curiosity and even pride. It seems strange to me that I hadn't paid more attention to them earlier. They please me just like an unexpected gift - a new, powerful acquisition.

25 June

WE PLAYMATES have been greatly dispersed lately. Most boys have left school and are doing fatigue duty at Maleme Airport. They are substituting for the adults who stay home to work the land.

In my father's place recently went my oldest brother - frail, sensitive, just a boy fourteen years of age.

Yesterday, at the end of his first week, I agreed – with some fear, to tell the truth – to take him a sack with a little dark bread made from barley and oats, along with some cheese, eggs, olives, and raisins.

The way, a distance of over twenty kilometers, is difficult because it goes across Rova mountain and I'm not familiar with the path.

Part of the way it is necessary to go on the motor road. There isn't a path. That section seems endless to me. The guardhouses, the road blocks, the dust raised by the heavy military vehicles in the road, all together create a scene of despair.

As the time passed there began to creep into my awareness a fear, sort of a resignation, that this wild unfamiliar area would slowly suck the life out of me and that it was unlikely that I would ever return to my own village.

To overcome this destructive feeling I tried to speak to anyone I happened to meet and to ask them something or other. I even greeted several German soldiers who seemed to me to have even-tempered faces. And they returned my greeting, with only one exception.

Two or three times I would speak into the air, just to enjoy the sound, as if the beautiful familiar words – ever-present friends – could by themselves keep me company.

I arrived at Maleme early in the afternoon, with my heart in my mouth.

The shack where the workers from our village stayed was empty, except for two sick boys who had been excused from work.

Thirty improvised pallets on the ground, ragged clothing strewn here and there or hanging on the walls, together with empty sacks, dampness, stench, and the coughing of the sick boys, all this frightened me. If those big tired eyes hadn't been watching me, I would have started crying.

The walls of the shack were filled with scribbled misspelled phrases: «Be careful of the carpet», «Visitors please wait in the living room», «Officials to the right, please».

An arrow pointed to a little door which led into the yard with an improvised latrine.

They had funny paintings on the walls, too. I really liked the one of a drunkard who with one hand was holding his greatly enlarged belly.

I sat and talked a while with the sick boys. I wanted to see my brother, to be sure that these miserable experiences hadn't changed him. But the day was passing quickly. I had to get on the road to head back. With two hours of quick walking I would be able to stop at a village on the way. I could pass the night there at Uncle Peter's house and then continue on home the next day.

And today as I write these lines, I have continually in my mind's eye that miserable damp shack and the memory of its awful smell. I also have an irrational fear that life there can twist human beings into something else. They could become limp slimy creatures who will not be able to stand upright, who will crawl on the ground, in the mud, and will no longer be human.

26 June

LAST NIGHT I again dreamed that I was flying high up in the air. It was an erratic, precarious flight. When I would see the chaos below it frightened me a lot. I woke up just as I was falling into an empty void, ready to be shattered to pieces. It took a long time for my breathing to return to normal.

There are moments even when I'm awake that I feel like flying in order to flee from the world.

At noon today I went by myself down to the river bank. I ran and spread my arms the way the swallows spread their wings.

Reaching the crossing, I climbed onto the plank that bridges the main stream. I shook the wood and halfheartedly ate big dark grapes. I tried to spit the seeds at the frogs basking with drowsy eyes on the mossy river rocks near the bank. With my bare feet I muddied the water around me. I threw stones and frightened the wild ducks and terns which fluttered with effort from depth to depth. With their lustrous bodies they made beautiful moving circles on the quiet waters.

That beautiful place was my first memory as a small child, a tiny tot.

My mother would come to do the laundry, and would bring me along, too. So that I wouldn't drown in the current, she put me into a deep basket, and ran a rope from its handle around a branch so that the basket would remain upright.

When I would begin crying, she would pull the basket towards the river so that I could stick my feet in the water, and play and not cry.

She always raised her dress up to her knees and tied it in the middle with a slip-knot. Right there at that very same washing rock, bent over for hours, she did the laundry while singing quietly.

If she happened to hear the steps of another person or the horseshoes of a mule, she loosened the slip-knot and let the hem of her dress fall into the water, to cover her white legs so they wouldn't see them.

When the afternoon drew to a close, she took a bath. As she bent over and brushed her won derful hair – a whole sheaf cascading down like a gentle river – I was anxious to see her face again. I wanted to see that it was her, and for her to smile at me so that I would feel secure.

27 June

TODAY Vangelis, my little brother, died. He got sick with some kind of infection, and without a doctor or medicine, there died a blond three-year-old boy, good-hearted, intelligent, and strong.

Everyone in the house is crying today. And our father, whom we considered unbending, showed his weakness. Something cracked in his inner self. His soul seems to have shrunk noticeably.

From time to time I look at my hands and move them to the buttons of my tunic and to my hair to check and see that I am still alive.

Toward evening I crept away from the house alone, and tried to laugh. I wanted to see if someone can laugh again when it happens that Death has passed very close to him.

29 June

AT LANTRO'S coffee shop around noon today a group of adults were talking about facts and fantasies.

Mathios swore that as he was going along from Saint Dimitri's cemetery one night at midnight – pitch black – he saw fire coming out of some graves. He thought he heard familiar voices but he couldn't make out the words.

He wanted to get closer to see what was happening. But his feet were rigid, nailed to the ground. Only with the sign of the cross and the «Jesus Christ will overcome» was he able to regain control of his body and take the road to the village.

They told other curious and unbelievable stories, but attractive like fairy tales. To me, the most beautiful and most convincing of all was the story of Uncle Peter. It showed the pure feeling of goodness which unadulterated intemperate truth instills in the heart of man.

«One day at the crack of dawn, I went out

while it was still dark. I had secretly taken my father's carbine and had come down to the river crossing to hunt before daybreak, before my father woke up. I was about sixteen then and I was still afraid of him.

»As I came down to the lower end of the path, I saw in front of me a huge beautiful woman. She was all in white, about ten feet tall, standing silently in the middle of the stream.

»I thought that maybe it was one of those nymphs who take away people's ability to speak.

»I wanted to speak, but I couldn't. My breath was not strong enough to make a sound.

»My hands trembled. My knees knocked one against the other so that I was unable to move.

»Yet I succeeded in slowly raising the carbine to take a shot at the ghost.

»At the very moment when my aim was ready, the form moved and I saw that it was a woman riding a white horse. Since the animal had stood facing me, and was drinking water, it had appeared like a continuation of the woman's body. Woman and horse together became an unnatural gigantic creature. I would have shot her if the horse hadn't changed position.

»I was about sixteen years old at that time, an impressionable kid whose imagination knew no boundaries or restraints».

2 July

I LIKE to sing loudly up on the hills during working hours. And I am not embarrassed if the whole village hears me. I feel that speaking exposes me and leaves me naked before all mankind, while song is a universal language, which puts on my lips the voice of the whole world.

But recently there have been so many people killed that wailing is echoing everywhere and I can't sing very loud.

Ourania cries for her child every morning at Saint Dimitri's. Afterwards she goes by George's olive grove, which is full of German and Italian grave markers. There she laments for others, for the foreign mothers who have lost children.

She says that the ground becomes light when some mother's tear falls on it. She says that unlamented blood becomes a poison that haunts the earth.

Many believe that she has gone mad, but I don't think that's right. Yesterday I listened to her words and they were poetic and beautiful. They entered into the depths of the world's curse and looked for balm on the expanse of heaven:

«Dear Lord, if it's possible, turn around and look at us and sweeten this earth with your countenance. So much blood will poison it so that it may start gushing a poison tear instead of water...»

7 July

FROM THE CRACK of dawn the whole village has been pouring out onto the seashore.

During the night whole swarms of bonito fish, thousands of them, were cast up on the sand and lay there quivering until they died.

It was said that they were chased by sharks. But Manolis Sfoungaras, an old fisherman, hesitated to give his opinion. Finally he said thoughtfully, «Perhaps it was like a stampede caused by an urge of self-destruction, which seizes animals sometimes. Who knows. And humans suffer that, too...»

For hours everyone – young and old – hurried around, panting and amazed. With two or three fish in each hand, they raised sand and seaweed in the air with their bare heels.

There was one boy, a twelve-year-old who hadn't found a fish yet, who ran around crazily, howling and complaining. He had a flood of tears pouring down his inflamed cheeks, and kept asking himself «why?»

With the rising sun a dry hot wind picked up, and stirred up more sand.

The people now looked like shadows. You couldn't distinguish anything except the eagerness that governed their bodies and their movements.

Just then the priest, Father John, appeared at the top of the ocean road and called to the people:

«Christians, Christians! Come to church. Come to thank God for the manna which he has given us from the sea. Christians, Christians!»

But the stooped shadows continued, deaf to his appeal. Only one or two women crossed themselves.

Father John slowly came down from the sand dune which he had climbed so everyone would hear him, and crossed himself. «Thanks be to God», he murmured. «I know that you will not be bitter, Lord. You know us. It was you who made us from dust and you know us well».

10 July

THIS MORNING we woke up frightened. A mechanized German column came rumbling up our winding road.

But they didn't come to the village. They stopped at the top of the vale and began to cut the trees: poplars, eucalyptus trees, plane trees, willows, age-old trees tied to the shape and spirit of our land.

It seemed to me very strange somehow. To my way of thinking, the giant trees were all-powerful elements. And for quite a while I had a hazy expectation that they would set in motion their giant limbs to smash the blades which were cutting them mercilessly. But nothing happened. I understood that this natural paradise was part of another world, friendlier than man, less susceptible to evil.

The stories about vengeful ghosts which live in the bodies of the giant trees don't appear to be turning out true today. And that discovery leaves a bad taste in my mouth.

By evening the vale had been stripped of its life and beauty.

Many tree trunks fell into the bed of the river with an angry thump, spreading waves to the shores and giant fountains of water into the sky.

Small fish, eels and crabs, with desperate thrashing came out of the water and then sank back, finding the main current and fleeing to the sea.

The trailing vines, the wild roses, and the periwinkle creepers lost the trees which had supported them. They were strewn around on the ground in scraggly strands, with mixed-up leaves – playthings of the wind.

Some waterfowl returned at sunset, but they didn't stand dreamily on one foot like before. They lit on the lower rocks with both feet, distracted and with a wary expression, ready to take off.

16 July

THE WAR'S whirlwind has deposited five or six strange people in our village.

All of them are different, misfits in this village. Their dialect sounds artificial and comical. And their bearing seems too frail for withstanding the blows of this wild time.

Most approachable of all, for us kids, is Kontis Vasilakis. He is an undersized round-shouldered fellow, with a triangular dirty face and with bushy uncombed blond hair and beard.

In his expression and his actions it's hard to tell the difference between man and woman, as if his gender wasn't certain. It is difficult to say whether he is closer to being an angel or a demon.

Behind his thick glasses move two small eyes, quick as birds. His eyes are not in keeping with the rest of his face, which is always meditative but also with a shadow of fear towards the world.

He has peculiar ideas about everything. He takes kids seriously, even the toddlers, and talks to them as equal to equal. Yesterday he advised us to trim our copybooks to give their pages pretty shapes. «Rectangles are for gravestones», he told us. He became very upset at a simple essay assignment dealing with the economy, assigned by the sixth-grade teacher. «That theme is fine for ants and dung beetles, not for real human beings», he kept grumbling again and again without changing one word of his comment.

The adults quickly labeled him a «crazy calf», pleasantly and harmlessly crazy. They didn't take him or his jabbering seriously, except when they wanted to tease him for a good laugh.

I forgot to mention how he had a bad personal relationship with Saint Constantine and passionately challenged his holiness.

He's an iconoclast, too. Today he defied Heaven, beating the icons of the Ascension with a hammer and calling out: «God, if these are things which you want and honor, show us here and now».

God remained unmoved by the challenge. But we kids were upset. There began to rise within us a crazy little wind which impels man to topple his gods from their throne, leaving him to feel like a little boat on the open sea searching for a safe harbor.

17 July

TODAY I went back down to our river bank, to the ruined wreck of nature.

Of the trees which the Germans had toppled, the largest was a plane tree. We kids had baptized it «Plane-tree of Minos».

They say that it had been spreading its branches for over a thousand years. At its huge trunk a giant cave showed its wide-open mouth, which was used as a hiding place as well as a secret school during the time of the Turkish slavery. In its branches could be found support for big climbing vines filled with grapes in the summer and fall, right up to the beginning of winter.

Near it a person could find shade, fodder, and shelter from the rain. I liked to day-dream about some strange scars and all sorts of carvings on its trunk – ideograms of life, bits of the spirits of those who had passed by.

In the area where the huge tree had dominated there was unattractive nakedness, an unsightly mess. For hours the birds came and circled in the air and left, scattering their mournful songs. But even more distressing was an old squirrel with one ear eaten away. He regularly climbed up on a stump, left over from the big tree, sat back and raised his paws in front of his nose. He would stay in that position for a long time, looking around with his wide-open eyes. He had such an expression that it tricked you into thinking he wanted to speak to you, to tell you about the tree.

18 July

TODAY allied airplanes bombed our village. We heard that their target was the neighboring vale containing the German encampment, an artillery and anti-tank squadron. But there was a mistake and they came two kilometers to the west. They struck exactly in the area where the neighborhoods of Drapanias are located. They dropped hundreds of bombs and caused a night of hell.

My brain was in shock from the noise, the dust, and the moaning of the wounded people.

With difficulty I found our home, with its broken windows choked with dust, and deserted. I found my sister crying alone in the yard, a four-year-old child with her eyes shut tight in order not to see, and with her hands glued to her ears in order not to hear anything else.

Instinctively I grabbed the child by the hand, took a blanket, and fled to the Aistratigos caves.

My body was shaking like a leaf and my mind had stopped working. It was a mental state beyond fear and desolation. It was worse than anything I have ever experienced.

For a long time I tried to spread the blanket on the rough ground and I couldn't even do that. Finally I fell in a heap and slept next to the child.

In the morning I saw that some woman from our village had covered us with the blanket.

24 July

TODAY for the second time in the same year German soldiers came to requisition animals to feed the occupation army.

With the president of the community and an interpreter they took the houses one after another. They looked at their papers and demanded delivery of the younger animals which had been registered earlier.

Little by little they assembled a whole flock of lambs and calves which they herded to the soldiers' make-shift slaughter-house. Young animals, pampered by the children and well-fed by them, rolled their large expressive eyes. They were upset by their new masters, and unaccustomed to their harsh language. Several of the animals had tears in their eyes and expressions of entreaty towards the children, and the children were crying inconsolably. The adults were ashen-faced. They suffered silently, knowing how much their home life was depending on these beautiful tender creatures.

We don't consider nor refer to our animals as «beasts». We have seen in them plenty of signs which reveal thought and logic, and even «character». When they're sick, and at births, except for practical medicine we feed them with bread, and water them with wine. On Epiphany eve, we eat the same food, the «cereals». Years ago a fatal epidemic threatened the village oxen with disaster. And then the priests and the community agreed to force-feed all the animals with the holy communion elements. The communication of man with the work animals comes from language which is age old, sacred. We use Ancient Greek words which mean «go on, inwards, upwards, straight, hold on, not this way, along the line» – parable-like words, thousands of years old, which in today's language are solid, pure gold and a delight for anyone to hear.

Near the animals we have seen the most understandable forms of the sweet mania of sex, the agonies of birth and death, the affection of motherhood, the desire for survival, gratitude – many of the really important things in life.

So today we lost priceless lives. Our hope and our resistance diminished a lot today.

29 July

A BIG ALLIED airplane crashed up in the Northwind hills, in the evening day before yesterday. I went and gathered ball-bearings and other pieces of strange scrap metal.

Oddly, I didn't feel any regret for the airplane or for the men who perished. Curiosity about the vast awful debris of the airplane, which was strewn over the whole hillside, for the moment stifled all other sentiments.

But I was able to stop for a little while and admire a British airman, a very tall handsome young man, whom the Germans pulled dead from the wreckage. I can't get him out of my mind.

The Germans saluted him, while the local natives wept with admiration and compassion. Germans and natives gazed for a moment, and looked at each other without enmity, on the lifeless body of the young man.

When the guards turned their backs, I grabbed some cartridges from the airplane's machine gun. The next day I sold them to the boys and bought bread.

Now I'm thinking about how all my reactions were strange and inexplicable. Somewhere very deep within me something was tormenting me.

My hand rested on the wreckage longer than was reasonable. At its touch I felt both pleasure and pain.

And the feeling of the ashes on my bare feet produced in me a peculiar uneasiness. It was as though it was the remnant of a heavenly flame which came and died out in our area.

I wondered if perhaps that whole area of the catastrophe was sacred, not accessible for everyone, and that I was not supposed to walk there.

3 August

A SUDDEN flare lit up the small rocky hill east of our village at dawn.

The northeastern wind which had been blowing for more than a week had dried up everything. Now flames were spreading like lightning.

The pretty little hill was engulfed in flames as though it had been a mere pile of floor sweepings. Giant wild things perished with unbelievable speed: wild olives, flashy lentisks full of red-blonde pepper fruit, myrtle with fragrant blossoms, locust trees overloaded with three generations of fruit on their gnarled branches.

The women crossed themselves.

The men considered what to do, silently, motionless, with trembling hands. Only a word was voiced here and there. They wanted to do something, but didn't know what. Finally some of them took leafy branches and fought the fire for hours, but with no noticeable success.

All morning there billowed towards the north large swirling clouds of smoke. Among the clouds despairing birds fluttered. In the shadow below, terrified little wild animals were running for their lives.

Today our mountain is something to be pitied. It stands there in its wretched bareness, without any life stirring and without the singing of birds in its black skeletons of trees.

12 August

THEOHARIS' grandfather understands us kids better than anyone else. When we pass by his home he welcomes us, gives us a treat, and tells us stories.

Early this afternoon we found ourselves outside his garden and stopped to say hello. Evidently he had drunk a lot of wine, because he talked a lot and his eyes were tearful, and his sagging cheeks were red, as if they were ready to drip blood. Half of him seemed to be in another world.

Other times, too, I have seen men flushed like that, talking a lot, easily changing from laughing to crying, and telling their best stories because they tell them with words that come from an unlocked heart.

The old man began as soon as he saw us. But we couldn't hear him very well. It was the time of day when the planes from the small Hadzi airport ferried water for Rommel's thirsty army in Africa. Our ears caught scattered bits of conversation, especially those which the old man wanted to emphasize and so raised his voice.

«See that you jump ditches and cliffs to toughen your bodies. And that you work, work... When I was twenty-two, I diverted part of the river, there between the twin rocks, and channeled the water to the nearby vale. Pickaxes and shovels dissolved in my hands as though they were wax. But that time is past and gone. Night is coming. I feel I'm left behind. Now I neglect the farm and it neglects me. Let's call it even».

When the noise of the airplanes died down, he turned towards Theoharis and spoke to him enthusiastically, with some good-hearted pride.

»At age twenty-two, I stole your grandmother from the neighboring village one starlit night. She was only seventeen.

»I picked her up in my arms like featherdown, and ran through the gardens and marshes until we got right here.

»For the whole way she didn't say anything. Neither did I.

»We stopped there in the middle of the stream, with the water up to our knees. It was April and the water was still icy.

»I asked her if she wanted me to take her back, or to take her with me to the other bank.

»She didn't answer with words. She glued her body to mine, indicated that she was cold, and pointed me to the other bank.

»I was inexperienced, you see, a mere boy.

»I didn't know that a woman whom you've taken up into your arms through a thousand fathoms, and who hears your heart beating so strongly, will never say that she wants to go back...

»And see that you are a dashing man. Look high and far away, not low like a porcupine... See, we sat right here on this mill wheel that evening with your grandmother... She was as beautiful as a fairy in the starlight».

19 August

AT GALATA yesterday Fintikos died. He was an upper-middle-aged man who lived the two past years sullenly, with dimming eyesight, with the broken rhythm of the world inside him.

The first day of the German invasion he attacked a paratrooper with rocks and killed him, because the paratrooper was still stunned and groggy and unable to effectively use his weapon. Afterward he dragged the body and buried it beneath an olive tree, a little way from the village.

But that terrible deed never let him have a moment's peace. Fintikos couldn't shake the image of that handsome young man who passed into nothingness with two blows from his rough hands.

Little by little his mind went astray. Every day at noon he went to the place where he had buried the victim. He poured wine on the ground, left bread on the rock, and spoke to him: «Don't talk about what I did to you. I won't desert you. I'll come to bring you bread and wine and will keep you company».

And he kept his promise until yesterday. Yesterday, however, the fearsome deed - a mixture of bravery and cruelty, manliness and ruthlessness - after two years of causing him to sink into the abyss of insanity, finally broke his heart completely.

24 August

EVER SINCE early morning the atmosphere has had an unusual gravity. A dark cloud completely covered the sky of the island to the south. It more closely resembled a granite cliff than a cloud.

Angelis' oxen stopped plowing and shook violently as if they were trying to shake rain from their bodies. «A big rainstorm is coming», grumbled the plowman and hurried to finish the planting so he could unharness the oxen.

In the thirsty greenery the tenderer leaves reached up. They were seeking the water they found already in the moist air, before it even reached the ground.

With the first lightning the songs of the birds lessened and became wary. The birds flew a low quiet flight and fled towards the wooded hills.

Many insects changed color and stayed on the ground. Others jumped high and used the current of the land breeze to carry them away into the unknown.

A mule broke his rope and began to gallop away with his tail between his legs. His body was trembling as though an invisible horsewhip was beating it.

The raindrops were big, mixed with hail at first, and then plain. They increased so quickly it gave the impression that the sky was becoming a giant faucet to water the earth.

From the south came a strange blowing and thundering. The river was rushing down. The rain must have begun in the mountains earlier.

The water came down in waves. It dragged along dry leaves and branches. It swept down the reeds to the north, uprooted rocks and stumps with a terrible hollow roar.

Quickly it began to lick at the bank and to widen it. Now the little trees swayed with an unnatural shaking. The smaller trees collapsed and surrendered themselves to the raging stream.

In my spine I felt the same shudder which had gone through the body of the mule a little while earlier.

The flood revealed a new relationship between man and the power of nature. It showed him to be small; he became one with the terrified insects of the river area, almost a nothing.

29 August

RECENTLY rebels have struck German soldiers at several places in our area. German columns now make blockades in the villages, throw men in prison and shoot in cold-blood, wherever such attacks have occurred.

The villagers hide in remote canyons and caves to avoid the Germans' rage.

Yesterday a military detachment passed very close to the large cave at Harhaliana. It was filled with a group of women, children and old folks. They all crawled to the back of the cave and kept a deathly silence so the Germans would not discover their presence.

At the most critical moment, however, Alexia's child began to whimper. She rushed to it, took it in her arms and tried hard to pacify it. And she put a diaper over its head to keep the noise from being heard. But the child's uneasiness only increased.

Those around her grew pale and cast desperate glances towards the young mother. An old man got angry and glaringly addressed Alexia:

«Smother the child because - eh - you will destroy, you will cause the ruin of half the village».

«Have you seen many mothers smother their children?» asked the young woman with inexpressible sorrow on her beautiful face and in her voice.

Still clutching her child she got up and rushed towards the cave's exit.

«I'll go back to the village alone, and to whatever God has for me. Let the Germans kill us. But I will not do what even the wild beasts don't do».

Two or three women tried to prevent the agitated mother with whispered pleas. Just then the soldiers' heavy footsteps could be heard moving off towards the far end of the vale, to take fear and death with them.

2 September

YESTERDAY Vangelis Korkidis came by the village. He sat down to drink coffee at Lambis', and talked with two or three village acquaintances.

His face had changed and he looked much older than he really was. The worst sign of change was his mouth. It was missing the beautiful golden teeth – the work of a famous craftsman in Constantinople – which had given him such a charming and expansive laugh.

The congenial, now poor, wholesale merchant spoke awkwardly through his shriveled lips and avoided laughing.

One of the group tactfully mentioned the matter and Korkidis explained willingly and quickly, as though welcoming the opportunity:

«Recently Spyros, my oldest child, got sick with glandular trouble. The doctor advised me to get fresh butter and honey in order to fortify his constitution so that he would not get worse. There wasn't anything left for me to do. It was necessary for me to sell the teeth to Kriaris to save the child».

Here his voice broke and he stopped abruptly. But his expression had depth. And in that depth was written the perseverance of the pelican the time it punctured its own veins to give life to its near-death nestling.

The other men showed embarrassment and remained curiously silent. It was as though their words had completely dried up among them.

11 September

RECENTLY there has been a small topographical survey unit working just beyond the village.

A German, a man with gray hair, has come to our house several times. He also had a family, he told us, but he doesn't know what has become of them. Maybe that's what makes him seem weak and uncertain – a tree uprooted by the angry wind of war. So what if he's on the opposite side!

The day before yesterday he gave us an old colored blanket and asked us if perhaps he could sometime sit at our table with us at mealtime.

When we cross ourselves he also crosses himself, clumsily. Thus as we devour our food he clearly shows his satisfaction and acts humbly as though he were our prisoner of war.

19 September

AT THE EDGE of the water trough down by the plane tree, the old men of the village assembled and talked. They were excellent men: revolutionaries, Macedonian War veterans, fighters dedicated to national unity, people bitter over betrayed hopes related to Asia Minor.

They spoke slowly, deliberately, each one speaking in order, as though they were participating in a formal ceremony. They evoked earlier times with brief stories which often had great beauty.

«In the Macedonian villages where we found ourselves we brought real Resurrection. The enthusiasm of the village was exhilarating, frenzied. Have you seen priests kiss the hands of the common people? I myself was still quite young then. An old man in his priestly frock, with a white beard, pulled my hands to his lips and kissed them tearfully. And so I felt hopeless in my shame».

«We were here in the plain, outside the fort at Kastelli. Our standard-bearer – because of his impetuous haste – fell down a well and we were left without a banner. But suddenly we saw a tall woman wave a blue cloth to get us to run ahead quickly towards the place where the Turks went.

»She was one of the women who brought bread and water to the barricades. She had torn off her dress and raised it as a banner and rushed forward – in a shower of bullets – so as not to delay the pursuit».

«...We were a detachment of revolutionaries, five or six individuals. All of a sudden we happened upon the peacekeepers' commander with his soldiers near the chapel of Saint Magdalene.

»First the Frenchman spoke through his interpreter.

»'You need to make a treaty, because you are in a poor and desolate place without food, and you will die in vain.'

»Uncle Heraclis Halkias immediately stooped to the ground, grabbed a clump of greens and began to eat them.

»'We'll eat these, we will live and we will free our land, otherwise let us perish.'

»Instead of answering, the foreigner saluted him. Then he removed one of his own military medals and pinned it on Uncle Heraclis' chest».

22 September

WE OLDER kids have been taught that it is demeaning and dangerous to eat food scraps from the German camp.

They are the conquerors and we should not humiliate ourselves in front of them. We need to hold our heads high even if we are starving. Besides, they probably carry serious diseases, incurable diseases from prostitutes and other such «venereal diseases». The adults talk about these as though they knew them well, but they just fill us with questions and fear.

Even with all that, today I just couldn't stand the hunger. I went to the camp with the other kids and with mixed feelings of gluttony, disgust and shame ate whatever the soldiers gave us.

Hours have passed now and I still feel covered with a vague uncleanness. I'm nervous. Part of my good self has abandoned me. I'm searching for something, a catharsis, some kind of pure spring water to cleanse me, to return me to my former clean self.

23 September

THIS MONTH was a horrible one. Four village boys perished. Two smugglers were lost at sea just outside Tsirigo. One boy was killed at the airport where he was doing menial work, and one was blown up by a land-mine. They were all very special individuals and their deaths have drowned the village in grief.

And yesterday the elderly Christina died, the secret alcoholic with the red face.

At her funeral no one appeared sorrowful. The devil motivated people to tell bad anecdotes and glimpses from her life so they could snicker.

Most entertaining of all was her son-in-law, Gavomichalos, whom the deceased sarcastically called «Genius», when she would be arguing and telling people off in the neighborhood.

Gavomichalos offered a number of people glasses of wine from a flask. Then he himself drank a few more «to tell his mother-in-law good-bye», as he said, until he was really feeling high.

All of a sudden he threw the flask aside and with a very red flushed face shouted: «The hell with all these funerals. I'll sing you a ditty, to give the deceased a breather. Buddy, she was a woman who liked to excel – in love and in wine. Who told you that she wants to be mourned?» While saying this he also jumped up and sat on the fresh grave, rested his head in his hands, and with a passionate, long-drawn-out voice began singing a lusty song.

His wife seemed about to faint. But someone said that she was really just trying to hide the nervous laugh which had more or less overtaken everyone at the cemetery.

30 September

TOMORROW I will go to school for the third day. We have been jammed all together in an old Venetian building because the schoolhouse has been converted into an army barracks. I don't feel excitement, nor anything else I can describe.

The teachers are starving, with pathetic clothing, and their minds are not on their work in class. Their minds are somewhere else.

Only two new teachers seem to have taken inspiration from the difficulties. They work hard and speak warm-heartedly. They teach with such enthusiasm that it seems like a miracle in the midst of this generally gloomy time.

We don't have desks. The Germans dismantled them in order to make beds, rough mess-hall benches and tables. They burned the scraps. We sit on stones which we find in the fields. I am very tired from the long walk, you see, and a weak kid, so I couldn't carry a suitable-sized boulder. I have a round uncomfortable stone. The morning is very cold and I have to put my knitted satchel on the rock so I can sit down. But this makes my copybooks a real mess.

Day before yesterday Stratinakis called them «grocer's wrapping paper» and the whole class laughed.

I turned crimson. So much blood rushed to my face that I thought I would bleed out of my eyes. So I closed them.

10 October

OUR NEW TEACHER, whom we labeled «Mona Lisa» from the first day, has misunderstood my smiling.

«You're always laughing. Why? Do you see anything funny?», she asked me in a severe voice.

How can I show her my inner world? How can I explain to her that for me there is much joy and beauty among things that might mean nothing to other people? I enjoy words, school classes, thinking, even her shape. The weight of rocks, the new buds on trees, the patterns made by clouds, the whispering sounds every morning at school, the aromas of the fields, countless things give me pleasure. That's why I have reason to smile. It's too bad that she doesn't understand me.

I'm even puzzled myself at this good disposition which remains almost undisturbed within me. I feel like my soul has two layers. The sorrows of this wild time we are going through are in the first layer. The other, deeper layer is peaceful, invulnerable to pain, impervious to evil.

16 October

ARTEMIS, a boy from our larger circle of acquaintances, took his father's small boat, went out and vanished on the open sea. They've been searching for him for days. The women are wailing softly as if he were dead.

His mother gave me some hand-written papers which she found in his satchel. She said that if I would read them, perhaps I could throw light on something having to do with this trip of terrible silence. But they didn't throw light on anything. Rather, the mystery deepened. The papers appeared to be the last pages from some short story which shows very well Artemis' uninhibited daydreaming.

Uncle Argiris came back to the island after some thirty years of rambling through the vast oceans of the earth. The villagers immediately gave him the nickname «Old Sea Gull», but he didn't mind it. He may even have liked it a little, because he himself used it when he wanted to make fun of himself. And because he looked at sea gulls as old, life-long companions to whom he could talk in times of loneliness.

With the first rains the roof of his small house on the beach started leaking. But he was not worried. He was still strong enough to mend it. And he did manage to do so.

His great passion has been the small family farm, which now was all part of the German minefield, enclosed in barbed wire. He had been robbed of a great love, a great dream, and he suffered a lot from this. He had to do something, anything, to get revenge.

Of the several ideas that had passed through his mind, he liked one more and more. He toyed with it in his thoughts at night when he couldn't sleep.

This year the winter seemed to him more drawn out than previous ones. In his hut he looked at his withered limbs and murmured, «You old sea gull...courage...». His mouth – a red cavity – opened in a long drawn-out deep sigh. «You old sea gull, hold on tightly and don't become worse...»

In February he caulked the boat and painted it, changed oarlocks and the one oar. He even washed the sail in the river. He wanted it to be pure white. He tidied up the hut, as much as his feet could stand.

He thought it was unbelievable, almost funny, that he couldn't lift the wooden ladder to reach the topmost shelf. «Leave it till later...», he said ironically, but with no trace of bitterness in his voice.

The resignation in his face and the pointed comments clearly showed that he was waiting for something important, a special moment...

That night brought a wild southerly wind and earthquake tremors. Gusting wind currents from the Astrikiani gorge rushed down and flayed the sea, driving sheets of water everywhere. Out on the open sea there were tornadoes, and dense fog all over the crests of the waves.

Swallowing up a cloud of sand, leaves and small branches, the sea gave the impression that it would smother all the solid land.

The old man got up in the morning and dressed in clean clothes. Going outside he let his eyes rove over the wild horizon. His eyes alit on the chapel of the Ascension and he made the sign of the cross. With urgent firm steps he went down to the shore.

From the edge of the reed thicket he dug up two tins, over 100 pounds of TNT from «Teller» landmines, and dragged them one by one to the boat. He pulled the wooden plugs from their holes and replaced them with TNT detonators, closed the small hold and weighed anchor.

He didn't have to row at all. The fury of the moment drove the boat out of the inlet without sails, thrust it into the deep water and tossed it around like a dry leaf.

The old man didn't like being tossed around. He preferred to be in control. He started rowing, and balanced the boat to go straight to the north.

With a new squall the boat twisted like a whirlwind, bounced, danced and went with amazing speed until it disappeared in the ocean mist.

In less than two hours Cape Spathas was engulfed in lightning. And midst the continuous shaking of the headland could be heard the subterranean roar echoing from cliff to cliff, from ravine to ravine, giving an idea of what the end of the world might sound like.

The villagers who saw Uncle Argiris' boat leaving its mooring in such wild weather were puzzled. They didn't know; they didn't understand. Only one old lady – somewhat mentally disturbed – who was grazing sheep down from the old man's hut, murmured: «They're leaving. They're taking the trip of love...»

Artemis' story brought tears to my eyes and

gave me goose-bumps. But I didn't say anything to the boy's mother.

Today, three days after I had read the fearful story of the «Old Sea Gull», some fishermen from Kalyviavi found Artemis at the far end of Cape Spathas. He was half dead from hunger, and both his knees were seriously wounded. His father's boat, the «Agia Pelagia», was almost entirely ruined, due to bumping on the rocks during the wild weather.

In the hold of the boat, however, were still three huge antitank mines. It was clear that Artemis had set out to realize the dream of his imaginary hero, Old Sea Gull. But he hadn't managed to reach his destination.

I thought that this failure must have cost Artemis an awful lot.

That same afternoon I went to see him. In his eyes one could see a deep pain. It was the pain of those betrayed by life in their greatest and most beloved dreams.

23 October

ALL THE BOYS come and go to school barefooted, an hours-long walk, hungry, thin, most of them prematurely stooped.

On our path through the gully, we have left dense footprints in the mud, something like the tracks of sea gulls in the wet sand of the beach every morning.

Today we were taken completely by surprise when Haridimos, an only son, appeared with a brand new pair of shoes.

All of us barefooted kids greeted him with a stream of banter.

«Dip them in mud so that we don't cast the evil-eye on you».

«Give them to Lukoudis so that he'll give you an A in French. He wears the same size as you».

«Your dad sent word to us that you should wear only one shoe on each walk so that they will last you twice as long».

«Come, walk in front. From now on you will be our leader and we will follow you».

In despair, Haridimos took off his shoes and slung them over his shoulder.

In the evening at home he declared that he would not wear them again.

«Ungrateful wretch, I gave Marianos over 100 kilos of olive oil to get you those shoes», shouted his father in despair.

Finally they arrived at a truce. It was agreed that Haridimos would only wear the expensive shoes to church every Sunday.

26 October

WHILE cleaning a bass fish one of our villagers found a man's finger, half decomposed. It still had a ring on it, and engraved inside the ring was a woman's name: Judy Bright.

It caused a scandal in our village, throwing everyone into an uproar. Is it a good idea to eat an animal or fish which is contaminated with human flesh and blood? «Who will be able any more to –eh– be certain, here where human bodies are discarded on land and at sea, from one end of the world to the other?» grumbled old Periklis.

When they asked Father John, he responded in a strange, ambiguous fashion: «One needs prayers, lots of prayers, because a lot of darkness has fallen around us, and only God can sort it out».

But hunger appeared to be more powerful than the other instincts of man, smothering concerns and uneasiness. The fish was eaten, and laughing and teasing could be heard. But I personally now see the people who ate it differently. The scene makes my flesh crawl, as though I was looking at vampires. I wonder if I will ever again consider humans as pure as I had considered them before?

28 October

TWO OR THREE women of the neighborhood, together with my mother, struggled today to sew clothing.

They cut up thin blankets, tents, white German sacks, and a piece of parachute. They tried to manipulate the coarse hard materials in order to dress our thin bodies.

Threads are a big problem. They're inferior or rotten, and they don't hold together the coarse clothes, which come apart even before they get worn.

Regular material has been gone since the year before last.

From time to time we hear they are selling a few thin pieces on the black market. They are very expensive and most of them are rotten, because they have been buried in the ground for a while, and fall apart at the first washing.

My father does not buy from black marketers. «I don't want any business dealings with manure worms», he says to our mother when she prods him to bring something for us, who are almost naked.

Vasilis' mother, Aphrodite, sewed him a pair of pants from a white sack. On the back there remained a big «P» from the printing on the sack.

At school the bigger kids caught Vasilis and added two or three «r»s after the «P». Then they took him out on the playground, loudly reading the funny sound «Prrr».

Vasilis is furious with his mother today. He cries dejectedly and doesn't want to go back to school any more.

30 October

A SOLDIER, a boy about twenty-two years old, came back to the village last night. He had been missing at the battle-front since 1940. Everyone had given up hope of ever seeing him again, except his father, who was not quite right in the head.

As soon as he moored his small boat at the shore a German patrol shot him and he collapsed on the ground. He lay there until daybreak. The sand was soaked with his blood. Only in the morning were people able to take him to his home. He was still alive, but just barely.

His mother cried and laughed at the same time, while her whole body trembled. On her bosom the fingers of her hands were locked together so tightly that they had turned all white.

Around noon the boy died. He had only time enough to smile at his family once or twice. And he spoke a few words about the time he had been away:

In Serbia I dug a ditch under the wire with my fingernails and escaped.

In the mountains I was dying of hunger and ate bark from the tree branches, roots, acorns, and snow.

A boy gave me some bread on the plain and sketched on my boot a simple map so I wouldn't lose my way.

From Serifos I was in the water for twelve hours. My boat sank.

Yesterday before they shot me, I saw the light from our window and the tall almond tree in our yard.

1 November

THIS AFTERNOON I returned after spending more than three hours in the vineyards. I didn't find any leftover grapes, except for two or three small bunches. Most of the grapes hung hollowed-out from the tips of branches, along with the last of the winter figs, hanging the same way, ruined by the birds.

This particular time, when we lost even the last bunches of summer grapes, I felt something of a terrible fear gripping my chest.

All that remain now on the branches are sour and acrid: myrtle berries, sage, and wild pears. It is difficult for a person to eat many of them, to feel satisfied. «God has given us these things to trick our hunger», old Mathios told me skeptically yesterday, «and not to satisfy it».

For the first time I feel that nature is letting me down. And winter is crashing down upon us early this year. It appears to me to be a wild and boundless time which will not be easy to get through.

4 November

JUST RECENTLY they brought to our village a group of Italian prisoners with two hundred mules.

That greedy herd devastated our gardens and ruined the grazing in our small village area.

Even the wild greens, which were our daily food, were ruined. So there was a need today, for the first time, for me to go into the mine-field to fill my sack. My heart was in my mouth. Every stalk, every blade of grass, in my imagination seemed to me to be a trip-wire waiting for me, to erase my life.

It's unbelievable how much I feel the need for companionship here in this situation! When I see a locust jump on some dandelions further on, I go closer to it. It's a living being, a comfort to me.

7 November

LAST NIGHT Stephanos and I talked for hours in the moonlight. At night we always talk better, more openly. The excitement in our cheeks doesn't show, nor the moisture in our eyes.

«I am really worried about my clothes», he suddenly told me with a cracked voice. «All my clothes are old, in shreds. We are all pitiful except for my sisters. Them we have dressed. They even have shoes. It would be a disgrace to send them to school poorly dressed.

»'Women are the face of a family,' my grandfather says.

»At noon we were trying to figure out what I could wear for a coat. My father has a loose-fitting English army tunic with huge pockets. The front is so worn that it has changed colors.

»They have me try it on. On me it comes to my knees, and they tell me it'll do fine. They ask if it's okay. I don't want them to feel badly, so I say it's okay. But I'm ashamed. It makes me look like a clown.

»Do you maybe still have your old tunic? Wear it, please, I beg you, so I'm not the only one. Wear it tomorrow, if you can».

10 November

THESE DAYS I'm beginning to notice clearly how Mirto wants to talk with me and to always be near me. And I myself think about her a lot. These thoughts are so strong that I find it impossible to explain. Thinking about her chases away concerns and fears, with magical ease, and changes the face of the terrible time in which we live.

This afternoon she appeared at our door and was so different. It was as though I were seeing her for the first time. Out of breath, with her black hair sweaty against her temples and forehead, her eyes moist, with an expression which was a mixture of laughter, embarrassment, and fear...it was impossible to hide her turmoil.

«I want you to help me with mathematics», she said with a quavering voice, and quickly sat down beside me. So quickly that I realized she couldn't stand on her feet any longer, nor say anything else. Her hands were shaking and the veins on her neck revealed a rapidly beating pulse. But she appeared to calm down as soon as we started doing our math exercises. Afterwards we carried on an endless conversation.

I talked to her about hunting, about fishing, about working with stone and wood. I wanted her to know how I managed grown-up work quite well, as though I were not a child. It was the first time I spoke to another person so openly about my dreams.

But now that she was quite close, I began to marvel at the velvet look of her skin, the strong roots of her hair, the perfect layout of her eyebrows and eyelashes.

She talked even more than I did, about almost everything. She spread her life out before me so simply that I felt like she was giving it to me as a gift.

As she was leaving I went with her as far as the Aistratigos cliff. On the way back I hopped from rock to rock and along the ridges of the rutted pathway, intoxicated with happiness. Constantly before me now were her large moist eyes, filled with dreaminess and love. The whole world danced in those eyes, and only in them did it have real form and meaning for me.

The only shadow on my spirit is one question. I wonder whether it is proper for someone to enjoy such things in this severe, bloody time.

17 November

THIS MORNING, under the pine tree at school, the kids of my class were measuring the kilometers that they walked every day. The students from Platano do twenty-four kilometers just to high school, not to mention chores and playing. The others do somewhat less.

At noon I calculated my own walking. With one morning trip out to the animals I completed twenty-one kilometers. In the afternoon I again went to the river area where my father was plowing, to help pick stones out of the freshly plowed ground. I did about forty-five comings-and-goings behind the plow, seventy paces each. I got a pencil and paper to figure the kilometers. I didn't have time to finish before I heard Stratis calling me. He wanted me to come to George's field to play «little slaves». My mind argued against it a little bit. But the child within me very much wants to play.

So I left in the middle of the calculations and went down to the olive groves to play. The desire of the spirit won out over the calculating of fatigue, one more time.

19 November

WINTER is early this year and the north winds are blowing hard. Everyone in the village is hungry.

I have a suspicion that the powers of nature are being contrary, just to harass mankind.

The older boys taught me to make traps, using stones and slipknots, for birds and rabbits.

My dream now is to catch something so as not to go home empty-handed. With my first attempts my imagination and excitement went wild. I couldn't rest.

Since dawn I have been plowing barefooted through the bushes on the hillside and swaying on thorny paths. My heart was beating hard; you could say it was like I was about to find buried treasure. All of my senses, all of my being – like a wild beast – yearned for prey.

Today a big rabbit, just recently caught and still alive, danced like crazy around the branch where the trap was tied.

I dance, too. It seems unbelievable to me. I run home, realizing that I am carrying a treasure in my hands.

However, I do have one small regret, a small drop of pity within me for the wild beast's heart which will stop beating.

...But I certainly wouldn't tell that to anyone, because they would think me silly and childish.

2 December

ARIADNE, our village teacher, got sick and left last week. Her relatives came and took her home in bad condition.

Her warm, kind voice instilled what could be called hope and strength. And now we are poorer because of her absence. A sweet-voiced bird is missing from our sky.

As I was going along today outside the room where she stayed, I found two pages of a letter which she must have written earlier. Too bad I didn't find the whole letter. She talked in her own style about the school and the life of the village in these black times:

I'm looking out at the telephone wire where thousands of swallows have gathered. The younger ones try their wings uneasily. They are preparing for their big journey. For the first time I sense that I don't want them to leave. I have an inexplicable dread that they might not come back again.

Recently they took back the schoolhouse and made it into a barracks. They also have requisitioned the strongest and most spacious houses to shelter army services. The dilapidated house which we have fixed up for school leaks when it rains, and when the wind blows the children are showered by the dust which has gathered in the rotting stubble of the roof, underneath the roof tiles. The windows don't have glass, and as soon as they are closed it is dark inside. I wonder how we will get through the cold days of winter.

The day before yesterday I asked the central education office for a little paper for the school office. They sent me some old printed applications, blank on one side and with a few words written in. «Make suitable lines and use the blank side of the paper sent. In the future, all your contacts with this office must be done in formal-style language. Otherwise it will be returned as unacceptable».

The children are in bad shape. They have become coarse, hungry, and uninterested in classes. Lately in my fifth- and sixth-grade class there has been only one boy and thirty girls. The boys work in the fields, doing drudgery because the adults are not available. The girls behave like boys, talk menacingly, get together and have rock fights.

Frequently I catch them telling me lies.

The cynicism of the children worries me and causes me to lose hope. The day before yesterday a little girl fainted. When she regained consciousness she understood that we would blame hunger for her fainting. With obvious sullenness she looked hastily at us and said: «No, I'm not hungry. We have all we need at home. I simply wanted to commit suicide, and drank something, and I won't tell you what it was. That's why I fainted». You can't imagine how distressed I was.

Dear God, please erase from their souls whatever wrong you see that my weak hands have written upon them.

9 December

WE HAVE NEVER seen snow up close, here by the sea where we live. One of our dreams was that sometime we might touch the huge snowy covering of the White Mountains which in the east seemed almost as remote as the sky.

Yesterday evening was calm. The Maistros wind was blowing lightly and the sea was green. This morning we got up to a wonder in front of us - a world of new whiteness all around us.

A whole bunch of us kids, with wide-open surprised eyes, raced to see who would be the first to plunge into the soft white sea. We rolled around in it, and touched handfuls of snow to our flushed faces. We ate snowballs, and appreciated with body and soul this newly-experienced gift from the sky.

Strange that the vastness of the snow and the fantastic change to the world did not bother us. But slowly something like a sweet dream came over me: the snow was the sign of an all-powerful presence which in the blink of an eye could erase the work of man, bury evil and heal the angry wounds gaping on the body of the earth.

All at once, out of breath from playing, we stood like statues – pieces of the magical change in our world.

Sarantos, the most sensitive boy in our group, appeared to cry from the overwhelming thrill of the beauty surrounding us. I, too, felt a small but deep pain within me. For the first time, I sensed that the durability of man is restricted, even in matters of happiness and beauty.

20 December

LATELY we spend our evenings carving big pieces of wood, from the lemon trees, and making simple things: spoons, spinning-tops, spindles, paper-knives, ladles.

That's a consolation in the cold, silent, wintry nights. For the past few days I've been eating with a spoon which I made myself. That gives me a great deal of satisfaction.

Yesterday evening I decided to finish a tiny little mandolin. I was eager to find someone to teach me how to tune it. I believe I'll be able to play it, because I want to very much.

And something else I hunger for is painting. I paint with red geraniums, with wild mulberries, with colored rocks which I select at the clay quarry, and with the colored tiles from the houses. I paint with anything I can find. I love the shapes I create as much as if they were living. A part of my spirit is in them.

The adults, of course, do not look favorably upon pursuits which entice the kids and waste time. Our time must be spent in keeping ourselves alive. We pick up olives off the ground, gather greens, hoe, weed, tend to the animals. Even the small kids, with the need to survive, do their jobs. Bent over like ants, they gather wood, help clear the fields of shrubs and rocks, and look after the fowl and other small animals. The girls learn to spin and knit. The older ones weave.

The work takes all day and part of the night. How can there be any time or spirit left for musical instruments or painting...

But only in those sweet moments of day-dreaming do I hear voices and see visions of another world. Visions of a world which doesn't deny a child the pleasure of a musical instrument or of painting something on a piece of paper...

24 December

TONIGHT we went out caroling. For a good beginning we knocked first at the door of Aunt Georgena. She is good-natured, and always nice to us.

The tall shapely old woman opened the door wide and wished us long lives. But it didn't look like she was expecting us. Her girlish eyes clouded over as they searched the shelves and the corners of her home to find something to offer us.

Behind the half-door she put her hand to her mouth and considered. Then, with an odd step like someone hypnotized, she took her precious Venetian glasses from the cupboard, rinsed them, and poured water from the pitcher - just a little, as though it were an expensive drink - and offered them to us.

«Long lives, my children», she murmured. «I only have water. Water and love. Tonight we are poor. And evidently God himself is poor and powerless these days».

DIARY NOTES: 1944

DIARY NOTES: 1944

11 January

MY BIGGEST torment these days is the morning walk to school.

My feet are swollen, red from the frost. And when I walk on the gravel and on the big pebbles the pain is unbearable.

I wonder that some people write poems about dewdrops. Certainly they could talk about other things. For me, these frosty dewdrops are frightful and bitter, and cause a person to despair.

Every morning I cry along the way. But I'm always careful that the other kids don't see me and laugh at me.

Today I tried wrapping my feet with some rabbit skins and holding these on with string. Unfortunately, the rabbit skins and the string slip off my feet easily. I have to re-tie them every few meters. I just can't walk with them. Unfair troubles!

What a shame! At night I had pondered for hours on end over my invention and how it might save me from the great tyranny of these times. But it just didn't work.

12 January

APHRODITE is the most good-hearted mother in our neighborhood. She is a young swallow who shelters the whole world under her wings.

At the window where she sits and puts edging on shoes, she sings for hours on end. She talks and teases good-naturedly with all those who pass by.

Her seven children don't seem to be enough for her. That's why she opens her warm motherly arms to all of us, all twenty-six brats of the neighborhood, as well as others from farther away who move along our road, no matter where they're coming or going.

Lately, though, her inner world seems to be crumbling. Her sunny face has become shadowy, she doesn't speak much, and rarely sings. Her singing doesn't have words of love and joy. Joy is out of place. The times don't permit light in the eyes of humans. These are times of pain, of fearsome words, of mournful songs.

Aphrodite's work has died out because she

doesn't have any more animal skins. Her husband Nicholas does get some money from the automobiles he helps with. But that money doesn't buy much of anything.

The children cry for bread. It is a pitiful cry which their mother has no way to satisfy, a sharp knife that cuts deeply into her heart.

Aphrodite has become a skeleton. She eats hardly anything, so as not to deprive her children. As her body shrivels so does her spirit.

Two or three times she went walking and got lost in the Kapadoki olive groves. They searched for her for hours.

The day before yesterday our gang of kids found her, all curled up, stiff, without any expression, more like a tree stump than a human being.

Today she had gotten up with unsteady steps like a sleep-walker and went to the domed Venetian well at the main edge of the neighborhood. She sat on the well's edge, with a dreadful naturalness and composure. «Tell them how low man has sunk», she said, and suddenly threw herself into the dark chasm - nine fathoms deep.

You could hear the hollow thud and the splash of the water along with our cries of despair.

The men who came forward lowered Vasilis Stambolis with ropes which he tied to her so they could pull her up. She hadn't been injured at all, not even a scratch. But the look on her face, my God! Empty as the depths of nothingness. Her dress looked like it was glued to her thin body, which shook like the leaf of a reed – a dry stalk, without any life-giving fluid, .without hope of a new springtime.

16 January

TODAY, after two weeks, my mother made a little bread at our home. However, it has a lot of vetch in it. It's black, bitter, and soft like mud. When you eat a lot you get dizzy and sick to your stomach.

Bread is the most expensive, most sought-after item in our area during these years.

The bad winters, the land mines, the loss of the young men, the desperation of the war, all these caused production to dwindle, ruined the land and left it infertile.

People tried to prepare something which looked like bread and could be called bread. You could say they gave new meaning to the word bread. They used chestnuts, sweet potatoes, legumes, vetch, oats, chickpeas, whatever could be changed into dough.

Wheat is completely missing. There's barley in the black market. Hector works these days at Revithi, for one and a half pounds of barley for one day's work.

27 January

GOING ALONG today we found ourselves at Malathiro, the small neighborhood village which has been left without men. On the 28th of last August the Germans made a blockade, caught the men and shot them all. Only Father John survived, because the corpses of the others covered him, and fainting there he avoided the final death shot.

Also saved was a fourteen-year-old boy, George Kartsonakis. Before dawn he had gone out to the trap wires to check for rabbits and was thus outside of the German noose.

When he returned he found the village in an uproar. Before he understood exactly what had happened he found himself in the area where the arrests had occurred. He realized he was in danger himself of being caught in the net of death. But he remembered his father's advice, that if something bad like this ever happened, he should hide in a small hole behind the barrels in the store.

He quickly crawled on the floor and huddled in the narrow hole, keeping still as a rock. He heard the panicky voices and the choked weeping, the steps which faded away, leaving behind the terrible silence of chilled spirit and body. All this caused him to shrink and grow weaker, almost to the point of complete extinction.

And time seemed different as well. In the hours which followed nothing existed for him except a pandemonium of machine-gun shots in the ravine, mixed with the wailing and groaning of the women, and the croaking birds as they rushed, starving, into the small ravine which the young boy now imagined to be strewn with human corpses.

All at once he heard the familiar bootsteps of the Germans as they approached again. They finally stopped in front of the barrels, opened taps and began to drink wine. The meaningless voices and the wild laughing gave him the impression that he was surrounded by gnomes. Gnomes who drank blood and were getting drunk and bringing about the end of life and the end of the world.

And after the soldiers went away and only the

wailing remained in the village, the boy didn't want to come out of the hole. He didn't want to see the twisted world the way the gnomes had ruined it. Two women pulled him out by force, tearing his woven shirt to shreds in the process.

1 February

EVER SINCE yesterday we have been laughing about Petrantonis' accident. This clumsy loud-mouth had an expensive vice. He would drink, get drunk, and break whatever was in front of him, at the homes of whoever had invited him. The owners dreaded him.

The last home he ruined was Paraskakis'. Petrantonis ate, drank a lot, insulted Hitler and then, before anyone had time to stop him, jumped onto the table and danced on the dishes. He ruined everything. The women held their heads and ran out of the dining room so they didn't have to watch. Paraskakis grew pale, swallowed his anger, but didn't say a word. After some time, he managed to sputter, «mind only human heads, never mind about the damage, Antonis, my brother».

Yesterday evening they found themselves together at a house in Zymbragou. Petrantonis drank again, and got ready to jump onto the table. They were able to stop him, however, and Paraskakis suggested that they take him to get some sleep at a relative's home, who lived nearby.

The place was unfamiliar, there was a dense fog, and Petrantonis supported himself on Paraskakis' arm. They stopped across from a field filled with summer growth, sharp thorns whose needles cause pain like a bee sting.

«Brother Antonis», says Paraskakis, «there's a large pothole here in the road. We need to take off our shoes and socks to pass by, so that we don't get them all dirty in the water».

«Whatever you say, my brother», meekly mumbled Petrantonis. He took off his shoes and got ready to cross the «pothole».

Paraskakis, who knew the place well, took Petrantonis' shoes «so as not to lose them», tossed them among the roots of an olive tree, and then pulled him into the field with the thorns in it.

Petrantonis, dead drunk, started out through the summer growth and immediately began to scream for help. Paraskakis listened to him happily.

«Walk well, brother, to toughen up your feet so that you can dance on plates and glasses, even barefoot».

«Fear God, you lousy dog», screamed Petrantonis. «I am lost».

«Walk on freely, I tell you; don't be afraid; everything is just a habit».

How much we need the medicine of laughter in these times!

6 February

FIVE OR SIX of the village smokers are sitting at Raisis' by the plane tree. They're discussing and tasting various dry greens, trying to find possible substitutes for tobacco. They try sage, oregano, grape leaves, and roasted moss – wrapped in newspapers, butcher paper and old paper letters. They end up with thick clumsy cigarettes which bring a moment of enthusiasm and then disappointment or disgust.

One of the men curses the government which had prohibited the cultivation of tobacco on the island, with the explanation that our land and the soil is better used for other, more profitable crops.

The smoke's drug which had been flowing through the veins and cells of their bodies was badly needed... continuously.

And it's unbelievable how this craving overshadows all the other problems: survival of the family, hunger, lack of clothing, humiliation, diseases.

George Trahalis returned yesterday afternoon with three pounds of flour, wages for two days work pruning in Paraschou's olive grove. It was bread that six hungry children's stomachs were waiting for.

Outside his door he was approached by two young men who for some time had been conducting a black market in cigarettes, between the Germans and the local inhabitants.

With bleary eyes and trembling hands George gave them the flour and got four cigarettes.

Unable now to go inside, he lit a cigarette and slumped on the wall next to his door. The sun set, twilight came, it got dark, and still he couldn't find the courage to go in and answer to Antonia and his six children. A woman reported that she heard him crying with slow, silent sobs.

16 February

THIS MORNING at dawn the Germans again made a blockade. They circled the village neighborhood and put a guard at all the exits. No grown-up was permitted to leave. Only children could depart. And when we went by them they looked us over well to see if we should be allowed to go.

Our father, terribly anxious, said to take our few sheep and to slip out of the noose and slowly make our way to a neighboring village in the hills. We were to live there with a related family until we saw what would take place.

But how could we have the heart to flee? We dragged ourselves just above a little hill and sat there all day, with our eyes wide open waiting to see fires, with our ears alert to hear machine guns and the rending of people.

But nothing happened. The world was spread out before us peaceful and beautiful. To be sure, the peace and beauty seemed somewhat artificial, false. And the day was endless. It seemed like it would never be over. Our games were castles, trenches, wooden guns, land mines and graves – graves scratched in the soft soil with sharp sticks.

28 February

TODAY they also killed Manousos, the insane fellow of our village. Somewhere he found two hand grenades and took them with him.

His uncle, a doctor who trusted the Germans a lot, went to testify to them to defuse the situation. He hoped they might even send Manousos for therapy. But the local administrator followed the letter of the law about armed civilians, and ordered that our poor crazy fellow be executed immediately.

His sister, pulling her hair and filled with horror, grabbed hold of her brother and wailed: «I don't have anyone else» and «Our boy is sick», but she didn't accomplish anything.

When they pulled her away from him her bones crackled like dry branches. And she, blind with despair, ran and clung to the trunk of an olive tree and continued to cry out.

The death of the insane fellow caused us children a lot of grief. We felt like he was one of us. We laughed with him, we learned a lot of things from him about silly things and the secret world of adults, and he told us dirty stories. And when we wanted to persecute grown-ups, to get back at the big shots, we persecuted our poor Manousos.

12 March

A GROUP of village fishermen took me along tonight on a *pyrofani**.

We waited at Stomio for the Albona wind to settle and for the water around us to calm. Uncle Stavros talked «so that we could be heard by the weather and the spirits of the night», as he explained half-joking and half-serious:

«At a *pyrofani* the boat, oars, harpoons, everything must rest light as a feather on the water, so as not to disturb the order of the sea. Nervous ones are fine for hunting flies on land».

«Life here is quicker, more clever. It changes shapes and colors every moment and requires full attention».

The water calmed down before midnight and we let the boat slip out from Stomio.

Below the powerful light the water shimmered a little and the multi-shaped world of water seemed mixed up. In the muddy holes feelers and fins of the red mullet stirred, and raised

* *Night fishing, using a bright light to attract the fish.*

small clouds of mist around us. Two or three cuttlefish repeatedly changed colors and swayed gracefully on the mossy rock below.

Uncle Stavros took the harpoon, crossed himself, and told me to hold the oars carefully. In the stern the others were drinking raki with dry fava beans for snacks.

The old man struck with great sureness and accuracy, always with the same arm, and when he was sure his aim was successful he laughed like a child. But when he pulled the fish up, he looked at the victim and spoke to it softly and sorrowfully. His words are touching:

«Come, poor creature, I ruined your bones... I sympathize with anything that falls off the branch and can't get back again. I know about being an underdog, about pain. Those things are in life. That's the way it is, poor goose».

Dawn found us with a sea hamper full of fish, and with tired eyes.

At that time of morning the sea life was extremely rich in the shallows. But the old man says that we have to stop. We don't want any more. I was puzzled. He understood, and explained thoughtfully:

«The desire of man for excess will ruin the earth and will bring the end. This war and all the rest are caused by greed for more than is needed».

15 March

SINCE MORNING I've been dizzy from hunger. Around ten o'clock I passed by the stables of the Germans and decided to steal some crushed locust beans from the cribs of the mules, to eat them.

I was afraid of the huge mules, but they didn't bother me at all. Actually, one or two caressed me with their noses and warmed me with their moist breath.

I filled my pocket with locust beans and went to sneak out to the road. But at the door a German sergeant caught me. He pointed his pistol to bring me to a halt. Then he beat me with a reed, until it was broken into pieces.

I don't think I was afraid. I didn't cry. I felt something like a stone fill my chest. I looked around me for something, a weapon – no matter how crude – with which to fight back. My eyes lit on the rocks in the yard for a little, but I didn't dare bend over. The gleaming pistol and the severe look of the German fell on me with very clear meaning.

I left slowly, feeling a wild and vengeful spite. Many hours passed and the stony feeling in my chest wouldn't go away.

31 March

LATELY it hasn't rained for quite a while. Strong southeast winds dried the soil and caused the ground to have a thick crust with wide cracks opened by the sudden heat.

On the mountain large clouds gather like battered wings which change form and then leave with awesome silence. The sun really burns when it is out from behind the clouds. And it even burns when it is in the midst of the clouds.

The wind blew down the tree blossoms and unripe fruit. It withered human bodies and leaves alike, and scattered a thin layer of dust over all creation.

Everyone is complaining that they can't sleep and that they have headaches. Until today, it had been many days since the children were seen playing happily outside.

But tonight the weather changed. Thunder sounded. Familiar southwest clouds appeared on the mountain, not strange ones like the others. The first drops of rain washed the dust out of the dirty air and made a stain wherever they hit. Then pure rain fell and perfumed the earth.

We kids spilled out of the doors, looked around and knew what we wanted. We came out into the open to play and enjoy getting soaked.

Then the grown-ups came out. They could be seen cleaning the patios, opening ditches for watering the tree roots, taking out the animals to wash them. But we knew that the main thing they desired was to get soaked.

And when they called us to come inside so we wouldn't get soaked, their voices weren't really sincere. We didn't take them seriously, and we didn't answer them.

14 April

YESTERDAY I touched upon the topmost of human experiences. I teetered on the edge of the void called Death.

Returning from school, a bunch of us kids - breathless from hunger - stopped at Erontas' mill stream, at the blind river branch, to have a swim.

The water was super cold and took one's breath away. But none of us wanted to appear cowardly or weak by turning back.

However, as Andreas and I were going through the deep place, we got entangled, were swept away in the current and lost the last ounce of strength which was left in us.

We began to struggle, to grab for each other, and to lose contact with the air. One or two times I managed to reach the surface and to gulp air filled with water. Then my body became heavy, and my joints failed. It was impossible for me to go up again, no matter how much I wanted to breathe.

The golden reflection of the sun on the agitated water above showed where I needed to go to try to regain life. But I knew that I didn't have the strength.

I felt clearly that this was the end. It didn't seem terrifying. What worried me was the need to breathe.

These last moments left me with a little boy's grievance, with a feeling of absolute submission which thrust me into abandoning any effort at being saved.

The black water, the mud and the slimy moss toward the bottom were death. Above, the multi-colored iridescence of the sky, the feeling of the presence of the other boys, the fleeting images of the trees on the bank, these were life.

If life wanted me, let it do something to win me back. I had given it all I could. At any rate, I hadn't hated it, even with all its hardships.

At that moment, Elias, one of the bigger kids, grabbed me and pulled me to the shore. He had gotten Andreas out just before that.

They put us prostrate on some piles of sand, in order to get the water out of our lungs. Then they goaded us into going back into the water so we wouldn't internalize our fear.

My main feeling at this time was a concern whether this was a real approach to the edge of the void, whether this experience was completely genuine, whether it really had the significance which the other kids seemed to give it.

Today I know that it is the truth. It is strange how this fearsome adventure took hold of my thought without disturbing me at all. Indeed, I have an inexplicable peace. I look at people and it seems to me that I know a lot more about them. My look penetrates them and examines the fragile crystal of life inside their chests.

My relationship with the other kids is in a crisis as well. To me they seem fake, something like paper figures, without this distinct flavor of the end of life, like I had just experienced.

Sometimes I find myself dominated by a sacred pride over this touch of death which I sensed yesterday. I still haven't become accustomed to it. I exist in midair, dangling, somewhere in a void, somewhere between existence and non-existence.

28 April

NIKIFOROS the chauffeur returned from Hania at sunset. He was carrying a sack of bundled million-drachma banknotes with astronomical numbers printed on their varicolored surfaces.

Descending from the dilapidated passenger-freight bus, he shook the bag contemptuously and then dumped the bundles of money on the road, saying that no one would take them anymore at the marketplace. «Finally, I told a little pretzel vendor that I would give him the whole sackful for a pretzel. He jeered, and told me to give them to my wife to make me a pillow. Do you hear what that devil said?»

The village kids rushed and grabbed the bundles, throwing the banknotes in cloudlike bunches up into the air, yelling like a mob ridiculing a false deity.

The faces of the grown-ups were not all the same. Some laughed loudly, with satisfaction, almost vengefulness. Two or three currency lovers, still believing in their fallen idol, pale and uneasy, snatched bundles of the million-drachma notes to save them from the sneering frenzy of the kids.

And there were some who were embarrassed, with a shadow of fear on their faces. They kept silent towards this unprecedented collapse of money, money which until now had been accepted as all-powerful and indestructible. In the midst of all this someone remembered the prophecy of Father George, village parish priest in the first decades of the century. «There will come strange, poisonous times when the mothers will scavenge in the garbage in order to save their children. Men will throw money in the streets and no one will stoop to pick it up».

13 May

SOMETIMES I sit and gaze at the mountain which burned last year. It has changed a lot. Now it is filled with black and white patches, kilns of lime and charcoal which people hastily opened to exploit the remnants of the forest.

From a distance they look like open sores on the flesh of the ravaged mountain.

With the strong cloudbursts of winter new rock outcroppings appeared. The slopes are very steep and what little soil existed was gathered into rivulets and swept away into the sea.

The new rock cliffs stood out in the sun and they too took on a cold ashen color.

The voices of the wild animals and the songs of the birds, all the echoes of life, diminished. Before the fire, the partridges were so plentiful that in the spring they kept everybody awake at dawn with a pandemonium of clucking. Now five or six hunting dogs streak around on the bare ridges every day and drive them to the south, towards the inaccessible canyons of the high mountains.

Today the mountain glimmers and shows that the first showers of summer are on the way, brought by the southwest wind. The thunderclaps sound drier than before. They give the impression that they are hammering and shattering bones of the sick mountain's body.

28 May

AT OUR VILLAGE stores very early this morning they posted a paper sent from the «Headquarters». It said that death would be the punishment for anyone who spreads rumors or says anything different from the newspapers and the official pronouncements of the government.

«The Axis powers», it continued, «are preparing a final offensive on all fronts and shall crush all resistance of the enemies. Their final subjugation and the pacification of the world are near at hand».

«To hell with you, pigs», angrily snarled Manolas as soon as he read one of the notices. «They want to gag us. The pigs know that once the horse takes the bit then domination is easy work».

He slashed the announcement and called to the others in the rest of the coffee shops to do the same. But the others hesitated.

At noon the squad who had put up the posters returned. They saw the slashed places and rushed angrily into the coffee shop. They roused two or three passers-by from the village who were drinking coffee at the time and stood them against the wall, threatening to execute them. But Manolas stepped in front of them and told them that he had slashed the poster.

It seemed curious to me that they didn't kill him on the spot. Instead they fell on him with their rifle butts and beat his head and his chest mercilessly.

Manolas stood with stony, haughty eyes, trying not to lose his balance. Streams of blood spurted from his eyebrows and from the back of his head. And the blood had a beautiful color because it sparkled in the light which came from the dusty skylight of the coffee shop. That's the first time that blood appeared to me to be beautiful and strong.

2 June

THE EASTERN cape is a bare mountainous mass with huge cliffs in the heart of the open sea.

In the summers the sun bakes the stunted greenery and it seems as though the stones dissolve in the sweltering heat, turning the mountain a diaphanous blue, at one with the sky.

Lately I often go to the seashore area of the cape. I like to be alone and to think about Mirto. We look in each other's eyes every day. We know that we want to talk one with the other, but we hesitate. We know that the world around us is very painful, and it is really difficult to have the conversations that we would like to have.

And there's yet another thing that troubles me. Mirto is growing up much faster than I am. It is quite clear that she will be a woman soon, ready to follow her destiny and to leave me, still a barefooted boy, loafing at the seaside.

Why does life play such an incomprehensible game?

Today I am again sitting here on the rocks and thinking about these things. I observe how quickly my relationship is changing recently with the world around me. Hope is fading fast within me. It appears that I have definitely lost the era when I had the power to cheer up about everything. That deeper layer of my soul, the one impervious to pain, no longer exists.

A little way further down there appeared on a rock two wild goats. They are small-bodied, thin, wild kids. Instead of having water to drink, they sit hours at a time and suck at the sea air and lick the sour branches, to hold their lives together until September, until the rains.

I think that somehow, somewhere we are similar. We are waiting with a thirsty spirit for just one thing. They're waiting for the rain; I'm waiting for a better world.

Do you suppose the rains will come? I watch the goats endlessly to guess, and the strain causes moisture around my eyes and my mouth.

13 June

KOSTIS went to the monastery of Saint Paul the beginning of May. I wonder how being locked up in that narrow corner will suit this uneasy boy who up until now has shown that he doesn't fit in anywhere in the world. I know that his great dream was to become a writer. Do you suppose that he will give that up, too, within the walls of the monastery?

«Go and eat a plate of nourishing food, because you see how you are growing and you are pale and weak; don't get sick», his mother told him, looking at him uneasily. It was time to go; the boy understood and agreed with her. We immediately named him «the monk», but very soon left him out of our conversations as though he had died.

Yesterday, however, his grandfather unexpectedly brought me a letter. It was a stirring letter, touching upon things of the mind and heart which won't ever be forgotten. He wrote:

...We are three boys together. I came last. The monk who has taken it upon himself to instruct us

is a person from another world, peaceful, certain, strong.

With a deep, prophetic voice he draws us along through the concerns which tear the being of a person in two and shatter him.

At the noon mealtime and in the evening he speaks for hours on end about the mysteries of redemption. He methodically instructs us about the view that a world within us must die so that another world, more real and perfect, may be born. He reads old ascetic texts which speak about the roaring lion of the flesh, about the pleasures of the body which rot a person and work against salvation.

Patiently and calmly he reveals the mystical view of the face of God which the believer achieves with the purification of his body, his mind, and his heart.

Starting with easy-to-understand unrelated matters, he proceeds a step at a time in his teaching. He reveals how man turns his thoughts to the depths of his being and finds the light of true existence. He very carefully explains to us, with some fear in his voice and look, how to gradually control our place on the earth. We diminish our present intellectual world with obedience and humility. And we limit our present physical world with fasting, with calmness of movements and of voice, with breathing control, and with absolute reconciliation with the physical environment. That diminishing finally guides mystically to your harmonization with the rest of creation and with your share of Holy Existence. Quite suddenly you discover that you become the «Large World in microcosm», with ranges which surpass the ranges of the physical universe, because in you «God rules».

Tonight I got up at midnight and sat up on my hard bunk. I can't sleep and I am thinking. I got paper and pencil and am continuing the letter...

At the beginning I accepted the initiation into the monkish world with some curiosity. It seemed to me to be a world of good spirits, unable to disturb my connection with the other, the real world, and the calm within me. Big mistake! That calm world wasn't long in showing its fear of power, in increasing and in beginning to conflict with my old beloved world, which included in it Anna, the other kids, the dreams of travel and studies in a big university, dancing, parties, guns, wealth.

This conflict leaves me in shreds, without the power to make a decision or to choose a path. Which way shall I lean? Which of the two worlds shall I cling to?

From the washed-out look of Peter, who shares the cell with me, I understand that he also is going through the same crisis.

The monk follows us with skilled eyes. He approaches, speaks more, and counsels with a trembling - almost cracked - voice:

«The time of spiritual affliction is not for a man alone. He must approach others, speak, listen. He flees from bothersome experience. Spiritual wrestling requires quick flight. Entrust the problems to God and ask Him to find the solution. That request will always be granted.

»At the culmination of the spiritual crisis neither yourself nor prayer will help. If you are unable to erase everything from your thinking, keep it busy with simple mindless matters. Learn abandonment. The spiritual is the only worthwhile escape. We don't clutch the knife which cuts our hand, we throw it away.

»In the beginning escape is difficult. But with patience it can be managed. And if you learn to control - to guide - your thinking, you will have achieved the greatest achievement of life.

»In order not to bleed your spirit in this wrestling match, uproot from within yourself quickly, decisively, whatever holds you a prisoner of the world, and don't ever revert to looking back...»

I wanted to tell him how I am trying, but the old world still has all its strong roots in me, so that my spirit is wounded and bleeds.

In my despair I tried his thing about control of one's thinking. I didn't achieve very much. But I understand from the beginning that the monk can't be mistaken. That here is a healing strength and it is necessary for me to achieve it. I don't have any other solution. I only have doubts as to whether I shall make it, whether there shall be any strength left in me as there was earlier.

I ponder how this war of the inner world is very wild, and hurts much more poisonously than the visible war which most people are experiencing, regardless of how odd that might sound to you.

Sometimes I feel that my spirit is dissolving, that I am empty, a pot which cannot be filled with anything but pain.

I lift my eyes up outside the window, into the peaceful night, and let out a cry: «Dear God, why do you split the world in two inside of me?». But I don't get an answer...

19 June

THE RUMOR got out that at Kalathines villagers were gathering recently and planning to begin a resistance.

A large, powerful German army surrounded the area, caught all the men they could find, and shot them.

The scattered neighborhoods of the beautiful village were filled with black crosses on the doors and women dressed in black. The vast cypress groves of the area took on their other – their gloomy – meaning of a vast cemetery.

The utmost note of pain is felt at the home of our uncle, Efthimis Lirantonis, the exceptional violinist whom they also killed. They say that when he sat on his little balcony and played in the afternoon, he charmed so well with his bow that even the animals stopped to listen. The birds changed their songs. They gave off delirious sound patterns, melodies far beyond what one would usually find in nature.

His wife, Aunt Vasiliko, the sweet-voiced goldfinch who always shared his charm, his cheerfulness, and his joy at festivals, went mad. She collapsed into a deep silence and wouldn't raise her gaze to look at anyone. They took her to Souda, to a psychiatric hospital, and forty days later she died.

We visited at their home yesterday, scared and numb. We found the four kids, four shaky-winged birds who wait to hold onto life with crumbs from starving neighbors and with words of hope which all come from painful breasts and which are unable to console, unable to heal other pain.

A neighbor lady stood up to greet us: «Here was beating the heart of our village. Now we are without heart...»

27 June

THERE WAS a terrible explosion at 10 o'clock yesterday morning, in the steep seaside by the old chapel dedicated to the Virgin Mary.

They said that it must have been a navy sea-mine which got loose from somewhere and came and hit the rocks.

First we saw a huge umbrella of white water which went half-way up the mountain. Then there was a loud noise which shook the earth.

We, like a flock of birds, ran to gather fish. We arrived with the wild ducks and with the sea gulls, which nest in those rocks and were crowing down hungrily.

The rocks of the steep seaside were turned upside down, and had exposed to the sun its vegetation and its little animals.

Fish, crabs, and masses of tiny sea creatures were trembling against the bare rocks of the shore.

The deeper water continually churned up a cloud of reddish-black little fish. They were violently thrown up from the deep so that they formed a thickly woven mat. This writhing mat was so dense that the birds could stand upright on it for a moment to devour the fish, while croaking weirdly.

Much later a few bigger fish appeared here and there. Those of us who ate them suffered food poisoning. The fish had been in the midst of the explosion and had chemicals on their flesh.

The explosion had been extensive and had poisoned the water. For a long time it remained lifeless, and there was poison on the rocks that stank like dynamite, just like the rock quarries stink.

4 July

AT THE VOLAKAS home yesterday evening they played hoarse, dusty organs, and off-key notes of singers were heard.

For months now we hadn't had a wedding. There hadn't been a party in the village.

But yesterday when Vasiliko married, her relatives decided to «rob death of a day of happiness». Even though half the doors of their homes are marked with black crosses.

But even the widows and mothers of those who had died said to have the party. They didn't want everyone to miss the blessing of happiness, nor to let the village suffocate in grieving.

These same ones came out of their low doors with slightly raised kerchiefs so that all their forehead could be seen, and offered raki and sweet rusks to the wedding party.

There were heard best wishes and beautiful conversation warmed up in the depths of the heart.

And the table was full, for this era of poverty and devastation.

But Volakas, the wild giant who earlier could swallow and «digest stones», was now near starvation. And with the eating and drinking at the wedding he swelled up and died at dawn.

Everything takes a strange turn at our place these days.

6 July

LATE THIS evening we heard about the death of Alexander's daughter Emerald, a lady as attractive as cold spring water.

Two years ago she fell in love with an Italian officer, a prisoner, and wanted to marry him.

«Before you sully my face with this disgrace, put a bullet through my heart», her father told her, and put an old loaded pistol in front of her on the table.

She didn't say anything. She just gazed very slowly around the house. What a look that was! Such pain will never be seen in another person's eye.

From that evening the light went out of Emerald's face. Her actions, her expression, her words clearly showed that the world had nothing else to give her.

Last year she married someone in Rethimnon. But her spirit never returned, nor laughter to her lips, nor even the ability to cry.

Two months ago she got sick. The end came quickly and everyone felt better. We were delivered from the psychological pain which we felt for Emerald. It's strange. Death came to pull a piece of death out of each of us. He took those pieces of death along with Emerald and fled.

We consoled ourselves with the thought that Earth receives back a painful existence in order to sweeten it, to change it into a mended version... two meters of soil with violets, wild daisies, and silver oats.

10 July

TODAY I received the continuation of Kostis' dreadful letter. It is two fairly big yellow pages, folded and sewn at the edge so that no one else could read the painful writing.

I opened it and began to read with distress:

...This morning at a moment of terrible wavering I spoke to the Father Superior:

«This spiritual world, father, it seems to me sometimes that it is born of the imagination of man, fleeting dreams.

»Do you suppose there are honest men who accept it without tyranny, and they love it? Because you seem to me a man who is a little tired, a little worried...»

The look of the old man traveled far away as he sought for the words that he wanted.

«Yes, they do exist. And it is so much a part of them that not even death can make them give it up.

»'And others had trials of cruel mockings and scourgings, yea, moreover of bonds and imprisonment; they were stoned, they were sawn asunder, were tempted, were slain with the sword; they wan-

dered about in sheepskins and goatskins, destitute, afflicted, tormented; the world was not worthy of them; they wandered in deserts, and in mountains, and in dens and caves of the earth'».*

I pay close attention. Now I can listen and then think about it later.

In recent days I have learned to escape from the physical tyranny, to stop the spiritual friction within me which used to bring me close to madness.

In my thinking there still appear the pictures of the two incompatible worlds which had conflicted so violently and so unexpectedly within me.

My old world had the texture of the earth, the sea, the sun. Anna, the canyons, the intoxicating breezes of the mountain and the sea, the songs and the immeasurable voices of life, filled that life sweetly and beautifully. Sometimes I wish like crazy to find it again.

The new world of the monastery has its basis in the invisible range of the sky, in the flame of poetry, in the dream of perfection, in the deep, strong folds

---

* *Hebrews 11:36-38.*

of the spirit of man which is exiled on earth. And this world has awesome power. It has freedom from place and time. Just as it is unreachable! I'm not at all certain how beautiful it can be, though.

This simple clearing up of my thinking takes a load off my mind.

However, there remains the fearsome decision as to which of the two worlds I will choose to live.

For the moment I am a slave to both of them, I think. I need to do something, to take a stand somewhere. If I don't manage to do that, I'll endure the eternal misery of a soul split in two. And I will wander doubly exiled, rejected by both of them, an unnatural alien with no place to rest.

13 July

AFTER READING Kostis' letter, my own pain got worse. It passed the limit that the crystal of the human soul can withstand.

Day by day the world within me lies heavier and heavier. I search in vain for that deeper level, the water-tight compartment of the soul, which was impervious to grief and which kept intact my enthusiasm and joy of life.

At sundown I took the path towards the Honis cliffs, again alone. In the afternoon light the world had become smaller. The view was an austere icon, with the lines of the horizon, the almost artificial disk of the sun, and the snow-white chapel up on the dark rocks.

This evening the chapel bell did not seem sweet to me. Its sound stirred within me wild Byzantine shapes - all wounded.

I turned and looked at the sky. The smoky golden haze diffused the last light from the sun. I remembered Kostis' letter. Of all possible roads certainly the greatest tyranny was in the spiritual road.

Now I was in such a state that I fully sympathized with his inner torment.

I thought that I too ought to talk to God. So I let out a cry: «Dear God, won't you please straighten out this crumbling world?»

But I didn't get an answer. The sky was leaden. It was closed, impervious to the voice, the light, the look, and the attention of this same God.

17 July

THIS EVENING we were calculating the war victims in our village. We didn't even arrive at a complete list. We lost men in Albania, in the German invasion, in bombings, and many from land-mines - more than eighty - and most of them young men. Several neighborhoods, such as Nopigia, have drowned in grief.

Most of the houses there are painted a cold khaki color, a mud color, and the doors have large black crosses on them.

The women wear black kerchiefs. These are tied just below their eyes and around their mouths so that their voices come out dull, all peculiar and hard to understand.

Their hands are rough, chapped from men's work, the frost, and the sun's great heat. They are embarrassed to stretch out the palm of their hand to greet you.

The little girls are dressed in black, too. They are shriveled and withdrawn. Except their kerchiefs are tied in a knot under their chin and their mouths show. And their foreheads look better, too.

The boys are a bit more lively, with gray clothes instead of all black. Since it is inappropriate for laughter or playing to be heard in the village, the boys get together and go to an out-of-the-way ravine to play «slavery» and «war».

At the edge of the village a widow who married very young was spreading white baby clothing on the fence day before yesterday. At that moment an old lady who was coming out of the narrow street spoke to her in a cracked voice:

«Marigo, my girl, you should dye them a dark color. You don't want them to look like banners, like we're having a festival».

The young woman didn't speak; she just pressed her forehead a little with her black sleeve.

18 July

THE OVERWHELMING emotions of everyone can hardly be described today. On the radio they heard that the war is ending, that the Germans are continuously surrendering, and that we will come out of this hell.

This evening, huddled in my bed, I tried to sleep. But first I had to calm my excited thoughts. They were continually bringing up pictures of explosions, destruction, blood.

I steered my imagination towards gardens, to the bottom of the calm sea, to the bank of the river. I searched for magical pictures that could capture – even for a little while – my thoughts and imagination, and bring me peace. I had a hard time, though. I felt that the wildness of the times had been tampering with my mind and even parts of my soul.

One time I snatched the imaginary picture of a big red flower. I tried hard to fix my thoughts on it so I'd feel better. Unsuccessful effort! The petals of the flower split into fiery tongues. And then from its pistil came black smoke like that given off by the land-mines in our area when they exploded.

19 July

A WELL-BUILT middle-aged stranger, with gray-black hair and large wide-open eyes, wandered around the village yesterday and today. He talked with lots of people, especially the young people.

His slow strides betrayed a fierceness of spirit. Something made you anticipate that after two or three steps he would give a big leap, for no reason at all.

In the evening he was sitting at Skaros' coffee shop. A lot of the village locals gathered and he must have been talking about important things. Everyone followed him with great care and rarely spoke back to him.

They were sipping wine, and had given us kids the signal that we should not come near. But we would pass by casually. And out of the corner of our ears we heard words and read their lips about matters related to rebellion, guns, Germans.

With the conversation and the wine their faces lit up and their eyes moistened. The stranger was the first one to start an old Cretan folk song:

Eat and drink, gentlemen, and I will tell you
About a young man whom I saw hunting through the plains

....

Countries and villages look at him and they admire him.
The youth is not hunting rabbits, he is not hunting wild goats
Queen Freedom's tower is what has attracted his ardor...

The men's voices of the group as they sang along made the window panes rattle... a creepy instrumental accompaniment to the great song.

They sang folk Cretan couplets, epics, eulogies of bravery and courage.

I thought that I would remember everything. But today I realize with sorrow that they only come halfway back into my memory. Only one do I remember completely:

All the good things of the world are written in ink
But Freedom asks for a script written in blood from our own heart.

The words, the songs, the fire in their eyes...it was as though the youth of the village were made drunk with strong drink that evening. They walked and talked differently. Many of them abandoned their hoes and plows, and during the weekend took to the mountains.

4 August

IN RECENT DAYS, quite suddenly, the Germans left their border encampments and gathered in a circle around Hania. They exploded blockhouses, blew up giant coastal canons and spread immeasurable quantities of ruined guns, shells, and cartridge cases in front of our astonished eyes.

All of that steel world was cut into shreds in less than one day.

Our village was in a free belt below the hill which the Germans held. They waited with uneasy anticipation, sleepless and forbidding more than ever, something like a huge wounded snake which didn't know where exactly to put its poison.

The locals didn't lose even one hour. They gathered in various prearranged meeting places. There they formed into squads and fled to the mountains, to be organized into larger units to fight the Germans.

Five or six of us boys decided to walk as far as Koleni where there was a big exchange of guns and cartridges, to see that new guerrilla army.

We were not impressed.

Inside and outside of the inn men were milling around. They were ragged peasants with greasy old guns, usually LaBelles or Mausers. There were two or three fellows with double-barreled shot-guns, and many others with giant muskets. Modern army rifles were really few; those carrying them could not help bragging and looking down on the rest.

At the moment, the only thing they were doing was taking rusty cartridges out of their pockets, in order to compare them with others, to trade them, or to sell them - three pounds of olive oil for each cartridge.

At one moment, quite unexpected, they began joking. A fifteen-year-old boy had appeared from somewhere. He was barefooted and at his waist there was a cavalry sword that dragged to the ground. Someone picked on him: «Just look at Despolis with his sword, ready to drown the world in blood, unless he defuses his ardor by cutting some cactus branches».

Inside the inn they teased an old man with

knicker pants, with knives and an old pistol in his belt: «You're a real wonder, old man. Just what is needed for photographs and festivals». The old man called them «ghost shadows» and «pansies».

Then they started making a game of battling. One would battle against another to see who was more skillful with weapons. They acted like children.

The last person who came into the store was a tall young fellow. He was just a boy, still with fuzz on his long face. And he had big round eyes like the Byzantine Saint Dimitris. On his shoulder he carried a Bulgarian rifle eaten away with rust.

«Do you have cartridges, Dimitris?» asked Kourtalos, wrinkling his bushy eyebrows.

«I have two. I don't know if they'll work. They were very rusty. I took a tile and heated them in the fire, but I don't know right now», the boy murmured thoughtfully.

«Those people who take two rusty cartridges to war are those who don't care about coming back, Dimitris».

The boy went, without answering, and followed the armed men who had already taken the footpath to the mountains.

When he went out-of-sight at a turn, I swallowed my saliva and it seemed sour to me.

I am sure that he went expecting not to return.

11 August

THE SMALL jetty which we had on the western side of the Kissamos gulf pointed northward. It was a good shelter from the west wind for the small boats and caiques which frequently sailed the open bay.

Early on, a German column came from Hania and proceeded along the main road to Kastelli. Our armed guerrillas crawled up to the hills to have safe positions. They didn't shoot the Germans because they feared severe reprisals against the villages of the area. They waited, however, ready to fight with them if they tormented the villages.

The goal of the column, as quickly became clear, was the jetty. Without delay the Germans set off explosions and blew it sky high. Chunks of the great cement blocks remained. Twisted steel pointed ugly fingers to the sky. It was like the corpse of a sea-monster half hollowed out by vultures.

Along about five o'clock this evening, a stranger's small sailing boat was being buffeted out on the open sea. As the wind gusted from the left and the right, the mast of the small boat nearly touched the waves. He had pointed the prow straight toward the jetty, but was slow in getting toward land. He appeared fatigued, ready to give in to the wild sea, and we were greatly concerned.

When he approached near enough and saw the ruined jetty, he very slowly turned and left. How we pitied the little sailboat! To me it seemed like a bird which came a long distance, but didn't find any place to rest, and very discouraged flew on into the night.

13 August

ON THE OPEN SEA, beginning day before yesterday, there was a big upheaval, a sea battle.

Some of the young men, swift and skillful at sea like sea birds, set out in a small boat and went straight towards the fire in order to gather the killed fish.

Today they returned with their boat really loaded. Bad luck! The fish were rotting on the way home. But they brought them anyway, for everyone to see. Maybe also because they didn't have the heart to throw them away. The fish were the fruit of their newly discovered bravery. And the boys had tied wet kerchiefs over their mouths and noses in order to endure the stench.

When we saw them and marveled at them, their tired eyes shone like they were aflame. They went a little way out towards open water and tossed their bitter hard work into the water. I admired their courage and manliness. And I saw that others felt the same way.

Only one very poor woman, with a large family to provide for, as soon as she saw them throw the fish into the sea began to cry hysterically and to run towards them wailing:

«No! No! It's a crime! God damn you! No-o-o-o!»

She fell into the water, but two young men caught up with her and pulled her out. There on the rock where they sat her, she shivered uncontrollably. And her wet dress showed clearly the movements made by the bones of her skeleton-like body.

Her expression had changed a lot. It was clear that she didn't know who we were, that she knew nothing about us any more.

14 August

FREIGHT ships from the Red Cross in recent weeks brought thousands of sacks of flour*. These were divided among all the homes of the island, manna of life in the desert of despair in which we live.

The young women rolled their sleeves up their strong white arms, crossed themselves and kneaded with enthusiasm, with expressions of divine gratitude on their excited faces. They kneaded tirelessly, twice and three times, until the dough was light and bubbling over the tubs.

---

* *Towards the end of the war, as soon as distribution of food, medicine and clothing became possible, the American People engaged in a gigantic effort to help the Greek people survive. Individuals, unions, parish comittees, war relief organizations–various groups of sensitive people from all America–joined hands in an unparalleled campaign of understanding, which might have also served as a pioneer idea to the goverment itself in its ambitious «Marshall Plan». This humanitarian mobilization must have been among the greatest war relief efforts ever recorded in human history. –K.F.*

We learned that this unexpected blessing is a gift of the people of America and Canada, a worldly paradise untouched by the curse of war which devastated our own world.

The message of concern and brotherliness by unknown people seemed unbelievably beautiful in this pitch-black time. And the plump sweet bread which spread its fragrance through the neighborhood had in its taste a great power.

15 August

THIS EVENING the grown-ups were whispering in our yard and discussing terrible things. They thought we were sleeping. But we pricked up our ears and heard far more than they could have imagined.

In the mountain villages the inhabitants dug up their rifles and day before yesterday blockaded the ravines and the mountain saddles.

A German column went to open the blockades. Old Marathos, who feared they would burn down his house, raised a white flag at his door.

But his son, an untamed wild steed of a fellow who had been rambling through the mountains for three years, was ashamed. He turned his gun and killed the old man. Then he set fire to the house and jumped into the flames himself.

Two or three individuals pulled him out to try to save him from being burned up. They saved his body, but the expression on his dead face showed that inside him there had been a burning world from some other invisible fire.

No one passes judgment. No one knows what to say about such a horrible thing.

16 August

THIS AFTERNOON Uncle Panagos appeared in the village market square with a freshly oiled Mauzer on his shoulder. «Time for games», he said laughingly to the young men who approached to examine the well-preserved old gun. And he added: «Old men have also to play so they don't rot away and get thrown out like garbage».

The kindly old man had warmed the heart of the village many times, not only with his stories but also with his own life.

One day the Germans came into the village and erected a gallows at Lantros' coffee shop. They were going to hang Manolis Kotsifos because he had not turned in the armed men - freedom fighters - who had pulled back into the hills around the village.

As soon as the gallows was ready they pushed the twenty-year-old boy under the noose. Then the officer in charge motioned with his gun for old Panagos to come up and pull the rope.

The old man took only one step, unbuttoned

his vest and shirt and offered his body to the gun of the officer.

On the width of Panagos' chest there were scars from Turkish bullets - costly evidence of bravery, engraved there from the beginning of the century, from the battles which liberated the island.

The German looked at him strangely, understood, bowed. He lowered his gaze and gave his followers the command to dismantle the gallows.

The pale - almost deathlike - faces of the people following the scene returned to lifelike color. They stirred and looked at each other - astonished shapes living a fresh new life.

I studied the old man now very closely. I looked carefully to find some distinguishing characteristic of his words, his look, his actions, to see what shapes his scars were. Somewhere must be hidden from me the costly sky-blue texture of fearlessness, heroism itself.

The old man showed nothing, however, of those things I was searching for. He is humble, with a gentleness in his manner which reminds a person of the good moments of small children.

He speaks well of everyone except himself. He has buttoned his shirt all the way up to the fold of the collar so as not to show his old wounds. Only his expression has an open, deep oceanic look which contains the whole world and something beyond that.

17 August

YESTERDAY Kostis returned from the monastery. His unexpected return brought us something like the joy and fear of receiving someone raised from the dead. With beautiful, somewhat confused words - it's the truth - he tried to describe his escape for us. In the afternoon he gave me a page from something similar to a diary which he writes in, a page beautiful and strong, as always:

I had a chance to talk openly with Peter. All during the time of my internal struggle our conversation was dry, of few words, almost unreal. I believe that the pain beyond a certain limit dries up a person's humanity and reduces him to silence.

Yesterday, though, we started a long and real conversation.

«Peter, will you stay here forever?» I asked him at a moment, suspicious and almost certain that he would answer affirmatively.

«Yes», Peter answered without hesitation but with a tone of hidden melancholy in his voice. Something like the voice of people who are leaving for other, far away, unknown places, and their voice

has the sound of a permanent good-bye.

That tone of melancholy stirred a rebellion within me.

«I am leaving», I told him without really thinking. «I am going back to the village. Do you want me to say anything to your mother? I'll come back to see you. I'll come».

Peter was in the midst of a deep meditation and didn't answer me. He seemed to be suffering and I didn't speak to him again. I got up and took a few hesitant steps. I quickly took down my sack from the cell's wall. I stopped at the door. Peter looked towards me but I don't think he really saw me. I slammed the door hard, like you would lock the door against some bitter, unwanted paradise, and slipped into the other shadows of the mountain, into the small noises of the night.

My steps speeded up as soon as I was on the path to the village, and I breathed loudly. You might say that this same mountain had carried me away and now I needed to escape from it.

As soon as I drew near to the village a thousand pictures were confused inside of me: our house, the school, the company in the village, the monastery. The two worlds which were trying every now and then to start a fight within me.

I found peace in the idea that these worlds are created by God to exist together, to be a unity, and that even I have something to do with that fearsome task.

At one moment I had a strange concern. What are the village kids like now? Do you suppose we can talk together now that this fearful testing of the spirit has come into my life? And will they be able to understand even a little of the depths of human «being» which I have experienced this summer?

It made me feel bad to realize how very difficult it would be to describe these things. It is a treasury of blood which you are sentenced to carry buried deep within you for your whole life.

20 August

TODAY around ten o'clock in the morning the Germans opened an encampment of Italian prisoners at Episkopi and freed them. It was a whole battalion.

They told them to proceed in single file until they reached the free villages where they could ask the inhabitants for asylum. But as soon as the Italians had gone a little way the Germans without provocation assaulted them with mortars and machine guns.

Many lay in the road. In our village there arrived a bleeding horde, with ragged clothing, with little wooden boxes on their feet for shoes, with eyes already half dead from starvation.

The women of the village poured forth into the streets to help them. Among the women was Aunt Yangena. She had lost Stathis, her oldest son, on the Albanian front. Her old face cried and cringed a great deal.

«Stop that whining and weeping; these are the ones who killed your son», fat Loukas scolded her.

But she neither answered nor looked at him.

She stooped over an Italian who was lying on the coffee-shop wall. As soon as he saw her he called out, «Mother, bread». A mortar fragment had burned into his clothes and the flesh on his back. He was at death's door, but that didn't stop him from asking for bread.

The old lady cleaned his bleeding back with a white cloth moistened with *tsipouro* liquor. She was crying and saying to him: «Don't cry, my son. Yes, I'm your mother. Don't cry. I have bread for you, and milk, too».

28 August

LAST NIGHT I dreamed again that I was flying up high. But now I didn't fear the chaos; I didn't fall. And in the morning I miraculously woke up with a new spirit. In one night some inexplicable power dragged the garbage of hatred away and made it appear distant and powerless.

I remembered the beautiful blood of Manolas, the sweet bread from America, the words of Aunt Yangena to the Italian, the sky-blue texture of bravery in the eyes of old Panagos, the return of Kostis from the monastery, all the fearful and beautiful things in words and deeds in recent days. Suddenly I felt that a wide crack had opened in the sky's leaden ceiling which previously had stifled the world and suffocated the breathing in our chests.

As though heavy chains were falling off me, I stood up for a moment and then rushed downhill towards the sea. I stood at the seashore and cast an inarticulate cry towards the sky which opened wide before me. I felt free from the fear and the pain of this terrible era and kept up the inarticulate yelling. I felt an absolute certainty that the sky heard me, that my yelling was welcome there, somewhere in its depths.

29 August

NICHOLAS, our neighbor, was himself incited to join the mountain fighters this evening. Part way up the mountain, at the shrine of the Archangel, our elderly teacher - a relative of Nicholas' mother - caught up with him and spoke to him with a choking wheeze in his asthmatic breathing:

«Nicholas, this war is not like the others. Courage doesn't count. Other things count. Those occupied with defensive positions in the Curves don't have a chance. And if you go, too, you are already condemned. Either you will be injured or you will die. You'll leave a beautiful home, children, and a young wife, without getting to enjoy them, and they will be left uncared for in the world».

Nicholas considered for a while and then spoke.

«You're right, teacher, but in my heart a different wind is blowing, and I'm not sure which is right. It seems to me that to be truly human my children and my wife need more than just my companionship. They need dignity and freedom. It seems to me that if I stop now to enjoy home life, I'll be like the mice who burrow into cellars and haystacks, without a second thought.

»Sometimes you would tell us, teacher, that we are trees. And that our branches are the riches of the earth and our roots humanity. You said that some rough times are coming when we wouldn't be able to hold onto both. And if we save the roots, we save something. If we only look after the branches, we'll only give enough bulky surface for the wind to blow away the branches and the roots, too.

»And I'm going this evening to save the roots».

The face of our teacher changed color and he spoke with numbed lips, with difficulty, as if he had been drunk.

«Nicholas, my boy, dear Nicholas, stand up there on the rock so I can admire you. Stand there close to the picture of the Archangel so that I can see how you resemble him now that you have broken your chains. Stand that I may embrace you, because you are free!»

EPILOGUE
(FIFTY YEARS LATER)

Most of the people in these accounts are no longer living. But in my memory they are all still alive, as clear-cut, unusually strong individuals. The mosaic of all their lives, if properly presented, could make a colorful and exciting book. Here are a few small fragments of that mosaic. –K.F.

VASILIS *(see May 20, 1943)* was trained as a vehicle mechanic and went to work in Hania, the largest town in western Crete. In 1950 he migrated to Canada where he married, but didn't have any children. He never came back to visit. Seriously or jokingly he used to say that he would come back only if he became rich or famous. Neither of the two ever happened. Around 1970 a heart problem brought an end to his life.

DIGALIS *(see May 31, 1943)* died at age 92. His whole life was a real paradox. He was a joker at heart, a perfect story teller, friendly and generous to us kids, and particularly tender to the weak. However, he was frequently accused of having joined a gang of animal thieves. Usually brave but sometimes unreasonably defensive, he admired both saints and robbers. He both respected and hated the rich. He used to set fire to the brush on the hillside above his home, only to come back a few months later to plant trees and bushes in an effort to give the landscape its former shape. This list of inconsistencies could go on and on. My overall impression of the man is that he was not a mere person; he was a synopsis of the wild adventure we call human life.

THEOHARIS *(see June 17, 1943)* was taken to the hospital and managed to survive, in spite of a complete lack of medicine. His family was one of the families most heavily devastated by the war. His father was killed on the third day of the German invasion while defending their own home in the village. The home itself was burned to a cinder that same day. A couple of years later two of Theoharis' brothers, strong and handsome young men, were killed while destroying mines in the minefield along the village seaside area. The rest of the family were plunged into utter poverty and despair.

In spite of all this Theoharis grew up, made a family, and lives a quiet life as a farmer in a small fertile valley near his old home. He still has a limp due to burned-up tissues around his left knee. But that does not seem to affect his broad smile and friendly words to everyone that stops to say hello. The only thing that he never talks about is «those years».

PANAYOTIS, my father *(see June 19, 1943)*, lost his life when he was in his 80s, while swimming one June morning at the village beach. The chill of the morning, combined with his growing circulatory problems, probably made him dizzy and caused him to fall down and drown in shallow water, in spite of his being a good swimmer.

Apart from hard work, his most outstanding characteristic was honesty. Villagers who would disagree on dividing inherited property used to trust him enough to solicit his help, usually with a standard expression such as "whatever you decide is well decided, and we will abide by it." I never remember him telling a lie.

After the war, emigrants to America or Australia would often give my father a free hand to sell their small farms and pay their debts, money they had most of the times borrowed to buy the tickets to their new settlements.

A good friend of ours, Mary-Jean Irion of Millersville, Pennsylvania, wrote these verses at the news of my father's death:

ELEGY FOR A SWIMMER

No one saw him die that day in Spring.
The report was that he drowned in shallow water

just at the edge of the sea. Imagine that old
island man, that gray-haired, olive-skinned
and olive oil man, that man of oranges and
wine who loved the winedark waves, having
schooled his strength within their surge and foam –
imagine him going under there where children
paddle.

Rooted in deeps of mind, these summer nights,
questions sway and tangle green as seaweed,
restless, reaching up through blues to surface
in search along the reddening rim of time.
Rhyme like salt wind blows through morning,
bending the grasses, combing, listening, slowing,
filling the shells along the shore all
afternoon, shaping in their spirals, listening
under the tilted wings of seagulls, lowering
into the tinted streaks of evening, listening
lifting under the little arc of a fish
until, at dark, word hears itself curve
and turn, coming back at last and just in time:

Death called him walking along the sand.
He tightened and fell, thrashed into crests of NO

then calm as a mirror, let a seashell go
broken through his astonished fingers. Hand,
elbow, knee turning to crawl, he then
made for the sea, made for the rhythmic wash.
Giving his swell and fall to its suck and hush.
He crawled into the lap where life began.

KATERINA, Alexia's baby *(see August 29,1943)*, grew up into a big-eyed blonde whose beauty enchanted the writer of these lines so much that he asked her to join lives when she was 22, and so they did. A good business woman, an excellent cook and «protective mother» of two sons and a daughter, she seems to be coping successfully with human destiny: the eternal conflict between success and failure, grief and joy, hope and disappointment, and – through these contrasts – the arduous journey upwards.

SPYROS Korkidis *(see September 2, 1943)* grew up to be an adventurous young man. Not discouraged by his father's failure in business, he went to work in the Athens port city of Piraeus when he was only fifteen, and soon started his own venture as a merchant of electric equipment for boats. His small store grew quickly into a big, thriving business which is now run by the whole family. Spyros himself has recently come back to Hania, the place of his early poverty, where he has had a luxurious villa built on top of a hill, a quite explicit monument of a man's victory over his humble and ominous early life.

MYRTO *(see November 10, 1943)* was married to a much older fellow, a rich merchant in Athens, right after she finished high school. Following our strict social ethics of those years, we never tried to meet each other until she fell ill, 28 years later, from a serious nerve infection. It was only then that I visited her and tried to encourage her in her personal drama. In that visit she talked of nothing else but our school years. In her memory those harsh times were so sublimated that they seemed to be remembered and felt as a blessing. That same illness brought an end to her life three years ago.

APHRODITE *(see January 12, 1944)* without any professional medical help gradually overcame her psychological and nervous collapse and managed to reunite with the «conscious world». Her eldest daughter emigrated to Canada right after the war, and quite soon managed to invite and settle the whole family into their new home country. Aphrodite came back to visit years later, and it was a real wonder to see how much she had regained of her early optimism, her love for the whole world, and the somewhat butterfly and playful character of her youth. She lived to be 86 years old.

Sample Pages
from the
original Greek edition

ΚΙΜΩΝ ΦΑΡΑΝΤΑΚΗΣ

ΤΑ ΧΡΟΝΙΑ ΤΟΥ ΧΑΛΚΙΝΟΥ ΟΥΡΑΝΟΥ

ΑΘΗΝΑ

28 Αυγούστου 1944

Τη νυχτα ονειρεύτηκα πάλι πως πέταγα ψηλά αλλά τώρα δε φοβόμουν το χάος, δεν έπεφτα, και το πρωί ξύπνησα σαν από θαύμα με καινούργια ψυχή. Κάποια ανεξιχνίαστη δύναμη πήρε σε μια νύχτα σβάρνα τα σκουπίδια του μίσους και τα 'κανε να φαίνονται απόμακρα και ανίσχυρα.

Το ωραίο αίμα του Μάνωλα, το γλυκό ψωμί, τα λόγια της θεια-Γιάγκαινας στον Ιταλό, το ουρανί υφάδι της παλικαριάς στη ματιά του Γεροπανάγου, η επιστροφή του Κωστή, όλα τα φοβερά, τα ωραία πράγματα σε λόγια και πράξεις του τελευταίου καιρού άνοιξαν ξαφνικά πλατύ ρήγμα στο χάλκινο κέλυφος τ' ουρανού που στένευε πριν τον κόσμο κι έπνιγε την ανάσα της ζωής στα στήθη μου.

Σαν να 'πεσαν από πάνω μου βαριές αλυσίδες, σηκώθηκα και χίμηξα την κατηφόρα προς τη θάλασσα. Στάθηκα στο κύμα κι έβγαλα άναρθρες κραυγές προς τον ουρανό που άνοιγε διάπλατα μπροστά μου. Ένιωθα ελεύθερος από το φόβο και την οδύνη του φοβερού καιρού και συνέχισα τον άναρθρο αλαλαγμό, με μια απόλυτη βεβαιότητα πως ο ουρανός μ' άκουγε, πως ο αλαλαγμός μου ήταν ευπρόσδεκτος κάπου εκεί στα βάθη του.

29 Αυγούστου 1944

Ο ΝΙΚΟΛΑΣ, ο γείτονας, ξεσηκώθηκε κι αυτός για το βουνό απόψε. Πιο πάνω, στο εικονοστάσι τ' Αρχάγγελου, τον πρόλαβε ο γερο-Δάσκαλός μας, συγγενής από τη μάνα του, και του μίλησε με σφυριχτή πνιγμένη στο άσθμα ανάσα:

–Νικόλα, τούτος ο πόλεμος δε μοιάζει με τους άλλους. Η παλικαριά δεν πολυμετρά. Άλλα μετρούν. Αυτοί που ταμπουρώθηκαν στις Κούρμπες είναι χαμένοι. Αν πας κι εσύ, γράψε έναν ακόμη δικασμένο. Ή θα μισερωθείς ή θα χαθείς. Θ' αφήσεις όμορφο νοικοκυριό, παιδιά και νια γυναίκα δίχως να τα χαρείς, αφρόντιστα στον κόσμο.

Ο Νικόλας συλλογιάστηκε λίγο κι ύστερα μίλησε.

–Καλά τα λες, Δάσκαλε, μόνο που εμένα σηκώθηκε άλλος άνεμος μέσα μου και δεν καταλαβαίνω. Μου φαίνεται πως τα παιδιά και η γυναίκα έχουν πιο πολύ ανάγκη να τους δώσω έναν αέρα ανθρωπιάς παρά τη συντροφιά μου. Κι αν κάτσω αυτή την ώρα να χαρώ το νοικοκυριό, θα γίνω ένα με τους ποντικούς που τρυποχώνονται σε κελάρια και θημωνιές δίχως άλλη έγνοια...

Κάποτε μας είπες, Δάσκαλε, πως είμαστε δέντρα. Κι είναι κλαδιά μας τ' αγαθά της γης και ρίζες μας

About the Author

KIMON FARANTAKIS was born January 31, 1931, in Drapanias, an agricultural area of western Crete. He married Katerina Verikaki from Hania, the capital of Crete. He was graduated from the University of Athens with a major in theology, studied religious education at Lancaster Theological Seminary in Pennsylvania, and has also done post-graduate work both in Ancient Greek language and literature and in English language and literature.

He is founder and president of the Pyrsos Group of language schools, with sites in the Athens suburbs of Halandri, Agia Paraskevi, and Holargos, and in Hania, Crete.

He is past president of the Panhellenic Association of Language School Owners, and is the author of several books. His ***Rising Up to Fluency*** *is a modern approach for students of English. In addition to* ***Ta Xronia tou Xalkinou Ouranou*** (The Years of the Copper Sky), *his other books include* ***O Potamos*** (The River), ***Anthropoi kai Iskioi***

(People and Shadows), *and* ***Odhoiporiko se Kritiko Xorio*** (Explorations in a Cretan Village).

When they are not in Crete, Kimon and Katerina now reside in their country villa on Penteli Mountain east of Athens.

About the Translator

P. DAVID SEAMAN was born near Pittsburgh, Pennsylvania, on January 31, 1932, exactly one year after Kimon Farantakis was born. They met in 1969 when Seaman was chairman of the English Department at the University of Athens, and have been close friends ever since.

After serving in the U. S. Army in Korea, and marrying Mary Miller of Louisville, Kentucky, Seaman completed his Ph.D. in Linguistics and Modern Greek at Indiana University in 1965. He was professor of Ancient Greek and chairman of the Division of Languages at Asbury College in Kentucky before joining the Anthropology Department at Northern Arizona University in 1967. He has been a visiting professor and consultant at several universities in the United States and Canada, as well as in Greece.

His publications include ***Modern Greek and American English in Contact*** *and five books about American Indians.*

Seaman and his wife Mary reside in the Ahwatukee-Foothills area of Phoenix, Arizona.